MEDIASMART

HOW TO HANDLE A REPORTER*

*BY A REPORTER

DENNIS STAUFFER

MinneApplePress

MINNEAPOLIS

Publisher's Cataloging-in-Publication Data

Stauffer, Dennis
    Mediasmart : how to handle a reporter* / *by a reporter
    p. cm.
    Includes bibliographical references and index.
    Library of Congress Catalogue Number: 94-076327

    1. Reporters and reporting. 2. Public relations. I. Title.

PN4781.S73   1994   659.2   QBI94-20537
                ISBN 0-9640429-0-8

Printed in the United States of America

"FOREWORDS"

Dennis Stauffer has written a through, knowledgeable and interesting manual for the "talking heads" who have to deal with editors, reporters, producers and photographers. MEDIASMART is full of insights and offers the best advice of all: tell the truth. Stauffer knows whereof he speaks. He's managed to talk about reporter's frustrations without being preachy. And some of the examples he cites are chock full of lessons for anyone who's ever answered a reporter's phone call.

Dave Nimmer, Asst. Professor of Journalism, University of St. Thomas; former reporter, managing editor for The Minneapolis Star; former reporter, Associate News Director, WCCO Television News

MEDIASMART is expertly researched, well written, and should be of interest to a wide readership, hopefully by those of the media. Dennis Stauffer strikes a good tone. I trust his views will be heeded by several schools of journalism.

General William Westmoreland, U.S. Army (Retired); former plaintiff in $120-million libel suit against CBS

For a guy who talks for a living, Dennis Stauffer writes really well. MEDIASMART provides invaluable insights and advice in an area where people need all the help they can get.

Larry Perlman, Chairman and C.E.O., Ceridian Corporation

There's a knack to overcoming people's differences, especially the often intense distrust of the media. Dennis Stauffer bridges that gap of misunderstanding between newsmakers and reporters in a way that will empower anyone who's suddenly "newsworthy".
Ron Graham, President, Minnesota Better Business Bureau

MEDIASMART is a useful and authoritative book that will be a handy reference for anyone in business or public affairs who deals with the news media. It's written by a respected journalist who has had a wide range of experiences in the real world. It's full of the kind of inside stuff that reporters talk about over coffee, and offers sound advice you won't get from any other source.
Betty Wilson, Political Commentator, Minnesota Public Radio; former political reporter, (Minneapolis) Star Tribune

Don't "fumble the ball". This book is like knowing everything about the media: what, when and how it is done without taking a media course. It has powerful insight for those who want to get ahead.
Matt Blair, former NFL All Pro; President, Matt Blair Celebrity Promotions

MEDIASMART is a must have media survival guide. If you ever talk to a reporter, you should read this book. With it, the mystery surrounding the media is broken. Dennis Stauffer tells you the real story of what happens behind the camera. Don't let the media intimidate you. He has the facts that will give you the upper hand.
Tod Pritchard, Producer, KING-TV, Seattle

MEDIASMART provides great insight and an honest unvarnished look at the relationships between reporters and editors, and the people who would like to influence the news process. This book should be mandatory reading for anyone who works regularly with the media.
Dave Mona; Mona, Meyer, McGrath and Gavin Public Relations

Dennis Stauffer is a perceptive, responsible pro who knows TV news inside out. He's written a great primer on how to survive coverage by the broadcast media and much of his advice applies to print as well. He almost reveals too much about the way the media works and how we can be had.
Dane Smith, Politics and Government Reporter, (Minneapolis) Star Tribune

This is a textbook for newsmakers, news reporters and wanna-be reporters. It should be in every journalism school library.
Ron Curtis, Anchor, WTVH-TV, Syracuse, New York

Dennis Stauffer has provided both reporters and public relations specialists with an invaluable road map for doing their respective jobs. MEDIASMART should be must reading for PR types, C.E.O.s and for the reporters they're trying to outfox.
Eric Eskola, WCCO Radio News, Minneapolis

Anyone who may have to deal with the news media at one time or another, and that includes about everyone, will have definite use for Dennis Stauffer's book. He knows that he's talking about and writes intelligently, instructively, and–as an added bonus–entertainingly. When a reporter calls, reach for your copy of MEDIASMART.

John E. Simonett, Associate Justice, Minnesota Supreme Court; Chair, Minnesota News Council

ACKNOWLEDGMENTS

I owe a tremendous debt to all the people whose names appear in the opening pages of this book. They are without exception talented and busy people who were good enough to share their insights with me, and help ensure that this book is as helpful and clear as I intended.

Those colleagues who have shared some of their experiences with me, have also been an invaluable part of my research.

I especially want to thank my good friend and former assistant, Adam Wahlberg, who not only reviewed the content, but helped correct my spelling and grammar. I knew I needed an editor who writes better than I do. In Adam I found such a person.

I also have to note my family's patience for humoring me through a long multi-year project. It's one I'm sure they doubted would ever end, much less succeed.

Those to whom I owe the greatest thanks, didn't plan to be part of this book. They're the newsmakers and other sources who I've covered over the years. They've helped me learn my craft and, over time, to understand how reporters and sources relate to each other. Some of them are quite skilled. Others have made colossal mistakes–and perhaps learned something from them (If they don't still blame me.)

Where I name people or organizations, it's not with any intent to discredit anyone. I'm just relating the facts as I know them, and interpreting them as best I can. A reporter's ethic is deceptively simple: They did it. I just report it. That's my job.

ABOUT THE AUTHOR

Dennis Stauffer is an Emmy award winning reporter with more than 14 years experience in television news. His varied career includes work as a television anchor, producer, photographer, editor, radio announcer and freelance writer.

For more than a decade, he's been with KARE-TV in Minneapolis/St. Paul. He's a former Business Editor and is now Capital Correspondent, covering the Minnesota Legislature and the city of St. Paul. Dennis' wide-ranging assignments have included everything from California forest fires to arguments before the U.S. Supreme Court, and from national political conventions to missing children. His stories have appeared on the NBC Today Show and in many local television markets.

He's also served as a media member of the Minnesota News Council, a body created to mediate complaints against the news media.

Dennis lives in Plymouth, Minnesota with his wife LouAnn, and their 9-year-old twins, Benjamin and Elizabeth.

CONTENTS

CONTENTS

CONTENTS

Dedicated to my parents Robert and Virginia, and my wife LouAnn, who–despite setbacks–have somehow managed to handle me.

PROLOGUE

You never know who may be piloting that incoming phone call. For me, it may be someone with an idea that will be my next story, or a complaint about the one I just did. Occasionally, it's been another reporter, someone who wants to put me on the other side of the microphone. If turnabout's fair play, then I guess I've been treated fairly. But I haven't always been thrilled with the story that results. One such call, I remember, taught me how awkward it can sometimes feel, when someone else is the reporter and I'm the source. A role reversal can be very enlightening.

It was not a call I expected, so I hadn't done anything to prepare for it. I didn't know the reporter, hadn't heard his name before. I was forced to take his word for who he was, who he represented, and what his intentions were. In short, I found myself in the position that I put other people in almost daily. For me, making those calls is routine. Being on the receiving end is not. He was asking me about a sensitive situation in my news room and I spoke carefully. I tried to sound cooperative, without getting myself into trouble, so our conversation was pleasant but tentative.

I knew I was a potential target for all the techniques I use to gather information and prepare a story, and it was a little frightening. I did my best. I made it clear that there were things I couldn't talk about, and at the same time tried to say enough to satisfy him. All the while, I was trying to put myself in his position, trying to figure out what he would do with what I was saying, and what the effect of that would be. I knew that ultimately I couldn't control what he would do with the story. I wouldn't even know for sure what the content would be, or how he would characterize what I said, until the story appeared– and everyone else saw it too.

As a fellow reporter, he understood why I was being careful. There was a certain "meeting of the minds" that didn't have to be spoken. He told me I wasn't the only member of our staff he had called and he joked, "You know, reporters make the worst sources." How true it is! In researching this book and talking to many of my colleagues about their work, I've been reminded of that remark. We approach each other cautiously, and for good reason. We know all too well what another reporter can do to us–and how it can be done.

This book is about taking calls like that, and about what happens afterwards. It's an attempt to explain all the things I would want my wife, my parents or a good friend to know *before* they have to deal with someone like me. I'm amazed that I haven't already seen a book like it. It's one that any good reporter could write. All I've done is take the same skepticism which we routinely direct at other institutions, and turn it on my own profession. Then, with a healthy dose of "how-to", I've turned it into *"News you can use."* Many of the things I say, are observations reporters make to each other all the time, but they tend to stay in the club.

If I have any added insights, I've gained them partly by serving on the Minnesota News Council. The News Council is a kind of Better Business Bureau for the media. It's a panel divided equally between members of the working media and representatives of the public, and it hears complaints lodged by those who think they've been treated unfairly by Minnesota news organizations. Sitting on the council taught me a greater appreciation for how the media are perceived, and how misunderstandings can occur.

Unfortunately, and despite noble efforts, what the council does sometimes comes too late. I've heard a number of complaints that I consider to be well founded, from people who have been genuinely wronged by a reporter. The problem is that even when those complaints are upheld, there's little that the council can do to correct the wrong that was done. Sometimes, it's a problem that could have been avoided if the newsmaker had a better grasp of how to handle the reporter (warts and all) in the first place. That's not to excuse the abuses reporters commit, or to blame the victim. I'm only suggesting that prevention is usually more effective than any remedy available after your story is in the news. Boy Scouts aren't the only ones who should "be prepared."

Most of the people you read about or see in the news each day, didn't plan to be there. News, by its very nature, is about the unexpected, and often the person who expects it least is whoever is making it. That's who this book is for: the legions of people–public figures and non-public figures–who find themselves on the receiving end of a reporter's phone call (or suddenly staring into a camera). They're people who may not have the luxury of planning what their public image will be, but who must nonetheless react to the public's attention. How you react can have a profound affect on the way you're treated, but it's a little late to start learning after the tape is rolling.

Professional media managers sometimes perform a service for reporters by publishing what's known as a "Source Guide". Typically local phone companies or universities hand them out. They list newsmakers, experts and spokespersons who a reporter may need to contact, along with their phone numbers. This book is a "Source Guide" of a different kind. Instead of a guide *to* sources, it's a guide *for* sources. My Source Guide doesn't tell you who to call for news. It tells you what to do when you are the news.

I make a few assumptions. One is that your intentions are honorable. I have no suggestions on how to mislead a reporter, and I recommend against it. We remember those who lie to us, and so do those who see and hear our stories. If you're determined to somehow take advantage of a reporter, you may learn a few tricks from me, but such an approach is risky and I think ultimately futile. An experienced reporter is a lot like an old schoolmarm; we've already heard all the excuses. Besides, deception is rarely necessary. We're amazingly easy to influence–if you know how.

At the same time, I don't expect you to assume that a reporter's intentions are always honorable. You'd be very naive if you did. But don't be too hard on us. If you begin every media contact believing that all reporters are corrupt, there isn't much hope for the relationship.

There are times when what I say will confirm your worst suspicions about reporters, and other times when I hope you'll be pleasantly surprised. My purpose is not to be an apologist for my profession, nor is it to write some critique on our many shortcomings. When you're face to face with a reporter, it frankly doesn't matter much how you or I think journalism *should* be practiced. What matters most at that moment, is how it *is* practiced. The important thing is that you see reporters for what we are, not for what you wish we were, and not for what we sometimes pretend to be. Once you grasp what we're doing, the rest is mostly common sense.

Staying afloat in the often uncertain waters of media relations demands skill, courage and a clear understanding of how to navigate. As with any skill, the execution ultimately depends on you. There are no guarantees. If you're looking for some impenetrable armor to protect your privacy, sorry, I don't know of any. If your goal is to gain complete control of the news coverage you receive, frankly you can't. What I can offer you are powerful techniques to influence how a reporter treats you and your story. The same principles apply whether you're a novice or a seasoned expert. They're techniques that allow you to be an active participant in whatever the story may be, not someone who just sits passively as waves of publicity crash over you.

As you read this, keep in mind who wrote it. I'm not a television news director, not a newspaper editor, not a media critic, and not a journalism professor. I'm definitely not *The Media*. What I am is the guy doing the grunt work out on the street. Reporters are the infantry of the media. That means we're who you have to deal with, on the front lines. Other people have important roles to play, and you may need to consider those roles. But the reporter is always your key contact. (Don't be confused by titles. You may come across a "researcher", a field "producer" or an anchor who's essentially doing the job of a reporter.) We're often the only contact you'll have with the media from that first phone call until the story appears. If you master that relationship, you've mastered media relations.

Hopefully you'll find my advice enlightening, whether you choose to follow it or not. Because by offering it, I'm telling you what reporters do and expect when we deal with newsmakers. Even if you're convinced that we're nothing more than an implacable enemy, I can at least help you *know thy enemy.*

CHAPTER ONE:

SUDDENLY YOU'RE NEWSWORTHY.

Discovering that you're newsworthy, is something that can happen in an instant. One moment your life is perfectly normal, and then, "Poof," you're a frog turned into royalty (or vice versa). It usually begins with a phone call, or less frequently with a camera at your door.

If you're already a public figure, you may expect calls like that. Someone running for office or building a movie career, may be praying for media attention. More often, it's a call to someone who's not trying to make the news. Maybe you're the CEO of a major corporation, the principal of a school, or someone who runs a child care center in your home. Perhaps you work in some agency, public or private, profit or non-profit. You may be a volunteer for some community organization that's suddenly caught up in controversy. You answer and a voice says to you:

"Hello, I'm 'Ace Reporter' with 'Everyone's News' and I'd like to talk to you about..."

It may already be the worst day of your life, and now somebody wants to tell the world about it. You may have just lost a loved one or been the victim of a crime. Or, you may have something to celebrate, but had planned to do so with close friends and family, not with everyone who watches the evening news. Maybe you're annoyed that a reporter would dare to bother you. Perhaps you're flattered that one thinks you're important enough to call. If you're like many people, your heart starts to beat a little faster. You feel yourself getting a little nervous. If you're like some, you panic, even before you know why we called.

It's a natural reaction. We've all seen those people squirm on *60 Minutes*. If a couple of reporters named Woodward and Bernstein could bring down the President of the United States, what will one of these guys do to me? We all recognize the power of the media. But all too often, people don't recognize that they too have some power when dealing with the media. You can influence how we treat you, if you understand what a reporter wants and needs, and how he or she will try to get it—in essence, how we play the game.

HELPING YOU HELP ME

There are three great lies, according to an old joke:

1) "I'll still love you in the morning,"

2) "The check is in the mail," and

3) "I'm from the government and I'm here to help you."

Given the public distrust of reporters these days, I suspect you could substitute "the media" for "the government" in that last one, and get a bigger laugh. Still, that's what I'm asking you to believe:

"I'm from the media and I'm here to help you."

Why should you trust me? Because I need your cooperation to do my job, and I know that the best way to get it from you is to offer you mine. Someone once said, "A reporter is only as good as his sources." It's true.

When I was just starting in the news business, I listened to David Brinkley address a room full of journalists. Someone asked this dean of television news what he thought of all the programs that were then starting, to train executives in how to deal with the media. The question was, "Is it making your (Brinkley's) job more difficult?" It wasn't the first time he'd been asked and he quoted himself, saying, "Heavens no! It makes it easier! It's about time they figured out what I need!"

After nearly a decade and a half in the news business myself, I wholeheartedly agree. The only thing worse than a source who won't cooperate is one who doesn't know how. If you don't understand how we select sound bites or quotations and edit them into a story, how can you learn to speak using them? If you don't understand our deadline, how can you help us meet it? Often, someone wants a story told, but isn't adept at dealing with a reporter. The result may be a weaker story, or one that's not told at all, and that's certainly not in any reporter's best interest.

When I have trouble getting people to cooperate with me, it's likely to be because they don't grasp what I'm doing, not because they know how to stop me—or should even want to. Often they do more harm to themselves than they do to my story when they try. I've seen many people become "their own worst enemy"—and make my life difficult while they're at it. Reporters love to tell each other our war stories, and there's one complaint we frequently mention. It begins something like, "If they just understood what I was trying to do..."

THE REPORTER'S QUEST

Dealing with a reporter has its risks. So does dealing with a doctor or a lawyer or an auto mechanic. All are people who probably know a lot more about their jobs than you do. And all are people who at one time or another may have some control over your fate. You shouldn't blindly trust any one of us. But since you may not have any choice but to deal with us at times, it's wise to learn as much as you can about how we do our jobs.

Granted, you have limited power over the situation, but the same is true for the reporter, and you're one of the limits we face. There are many things you can do that will influence how we tell a story—if you first understand what we're doing.

"Truth" vs. the "Story"

Once during a news conference with Minnesota Governor Arne Carlson, a newspaper colleague of mine got into an exchange with the Governor. As sometimes happens, the reporter felt he wasn't getting a direct answer to his question. He asked again, and still wasn't satisfied, so he kept pressing. Finally, the Governor in a tone of exasperation blurted out, "What is it you want?" To which the reporter replied, "I want the truth." (Score: Reporter 1, Governor 0.)

The clear implication of the reporter's answer was that he hadn't been getting the truth, that the governor was dodging his question. But the reporter's quick comeback was also something of a dodge. When a reporter says, "I want the truth," it's an honest statement; we certainly don't want to hear lies. But what a newsmaker really needs to know is, what facts does the reporter consider important? Frankly, we're not as interested in any "truths" that don't make a good story. Our job is to tell news stories, so we routinely select those facts that help us do that—and disregard the rest. If we do our job correctly, the result will be accurate and fair, but it will also be something that we have honed down to only its most interesting elements. Those elements may or may not be the most flattering to you. The best way to figure out which facts are the ones that we will use, is to find out what we intend the story to be.

The Governor may have been trying to hide information, or he may have been genuinely confused about what the reporter wanted. Only he knows for sure. Either way, he was asking what any newsmaker has every right to ask: *What is the "story"?*

We Never Have All the Facts.

When Mark Twain was a young journalist, an editor is said to have scolded him about the accuracy of his work, insisting that a reporter must be absolutely certain of anything he writes. Twain, the legend goes, returned soon after that with a story on a town social event, which he described as a, "purported party" for "a number of alleged ladies."

It's one of many stories about Twain that appear to be apocryphal–although some leading experts on Twain's work tell me it has an authentic ring to it. Twain was certainly scolded for his journalistic standards, which even he admitted didn't place too high a premium on accuracy. Whatever the source, the tale says a lot about the art of journalism. With characteristic sarcasm and insight, Twain's reputed comeback captures the dilemma we all face: If reporters are limited to telling about only those things that we can prove with complete certainty, we will surely say very little, perhaps nothing.

We have no more grip on the truth than you do. Objectivity is something we can only strive for, and fairness is often in the eye of the beholder. People who tend to think in terms of absolutes and certainties make lousy journalists.

I once spoke to a group of junior high students, who were visiting the capitol, to explain to them how I do my work. Joining me was a media spokesperson for Attorney General Hubert H. "Skip" Humphrey. She talked about her job of providing information to people like me, and the importance of making sure of its accuracy. She had worked in a news room herself and told the students that when reporters say or write something that is wrong, it's usually because somebody told them wrong. That's a far more charitable explanation than we sometimes deserve, but it's frequently true. We don't make this stuff up, at least not most of us.

As a newsmaker, you can't force us to do a story a particular way, but you can guide us to the truth as you see it. Sometimes you need to remind us of our shortcomings. We can always use some help getting the story straight. *Make sure the reporter has all the information needed to draw the conclusions you want.*

We Never Tell Everything We Know.

Saying that a reporter leaves facts out of a story is like saying that jockeys ride horses and quarterbacks throw footballs. That's our job. Every story involves choices. They're choices you may or may not agree with, but the reporter has no alternative but to make them. The issue isn't whether we're leaving anything out, but rather *which* facts we left out and which ones we included.

Like all reporters, I've been on assignments where I've been accused of not telling the whole story. Perhaps it's a piece about racial violence in a school. I can count on someone pointing out that most students behave and that the school has won many honors, "But you guys never tell people about the good things we do. Where were you last week when...?"

In reality we often do mention both good and bad. My story might include a quotation from a student saying,

"We just celebrated city championships in both football and debate. These fights really hurt the reputation of a good school."

Noting such contrasts can enhance a story. But the point is that there's a problem—racial violence. That's why it's news.

Every story has a "slant" or an "angle". That is to say it has something interesting about it—something that makes it a good story. It's the reason for doing the story. Some reporters call it the "so what?" test. No story should ever make it into print or on the air without passing that test for somebody. It's the difference between a "topic" and a "story", and it's how a reporter finds a "focus". Anyone can pick a topic and talk about it endlessly. (You probably know someone who does that.) The reporter's job is to cut through the available information to get to the essentials. It's a sifting process that is frequently misunderstood.

A few years ago a friend of mine did an investigative series of reports on welfare fraud–and was promptly accused of, "not telling the whole story." His series was based on several premises: 1) that welfare fraud existed; 2) that money which could have been going to those people who are legitimately in need, was going to others who weren't entitled to it–at taxpayer expense; and 3) that counties weren't doing as much as they could to stop such fraud.

The reporter, Rick Kupchella is the type of aggressive newsman who sometimes presses the limits of what some people consider proper, but he's no slouch journalist. If Rick was a soldier, he'd be called "highly decorated". (When I learned that I had won an Emmy for a series of mine, my natural excitement was tempered a little when I found that in that same competition Rick won *four*.)

Rick's series drew the attention of an organization known as Women Against Military Madness or WAMM. WAMM is an activist organization that includes welfare mothers under its umbrella of causes. The group felt that the series was a cheap shot at deserving welfare recipients, a story that didn't give the total picture and which unfairly undermined public support for legitimate welfare assistance. So, WAMM complained to the Minnesota News Council.

In a hearing before the Council, WAMM argued that the reports were biased, that they overemphasized the fraud problem, and perpetuated stereotypes of "welfare cheats". WAMM demanded that the station make amends by airing a more comprehensive report, one that covered the entire welfare system and the good that it accomplishes. The station responded that the series had included examples of the positive benefits of public assistance, and that we had done other stories that were favorable to welfare recipients. Still, because the main thrust of Rick's report was fraud, WAMM felt that it didn't give those other aspects enough importance.

The dispute ultimately came down to a question of emphasis. WAMM wasn't disputing the facts of the story so much as the way the station presented those facts. The key argument in the station's defense was simply that the reporter set out from the very beginning to do a story on "welfare fraud," *not* the "welfare system". That wasn't some secret agenda; it was the whole rationale for doing the story—and Rick's report said as much. That's the kind of decision any news room must make many times a day, when selecting stories to cover. The fact that a particular "angle" has been chosen doesn't mean the story is biased, or that all sides won't be heard. It simply means that the topic is being approached in a way that passes the "so what?" test. The News Council rejected WAMM's complaint.

In this case the "topic" was *Welfare*, the "angle" was *fraud–and what wasn't being done about it* and the "so-what" was, *This is a problem that is costing you money, and that money isn't getting to the people it's supposed to help.* If there's no "so-what?" the topic is not only a waste of the reporter's time, it's a waste of time for you the viewer, listener or reader. You watch the news or pick up a newspaper because you expect to learn something of consequence, not just meander through topics.

Distinguishing between deliberate bias and responsible journalism is often difficult, and the council's decision on the WAMM complaint was not unanimous. There was some concern among members about the station's motives for selecting such a story to do. Some personally disagreed with its premises. But most council members recognized that such choices by a news organization are what we mean when we say *Freedom of the Press*. If we don't have the fundamental right to select stories, without outside pressure, what choice is left? It's a principle which reporters loudly defend, as they should.

If you hope to influence the way we tell a story, you need to first recognize that making choices is every reporter's prerogative and responsibility. That doesn't mean you should capitulate to whatever a reporter wants to do. You inevitably have some influence over what a story will be, by the fact that you are part of it. You have the power to persuade, or even bargain at times. The important thing is to *Recognize that the reporter is going to make choices and concentrate on influencing those choices.*

You may not realize it yet, but there are many ways to do that. You're far from helpless.

YOU'RE NOT JUST A NEWSMAKER, YOU'RE A SOURCE.

The Mystique

Any student who's been through Journalism 101, has surely sat through at least one lecture on "sources." The professor starts by asking his students the obvious question, "What is a source?" Some bright student (with a minor in history) will say, "Deepthroat," referring to the famous and still unnamed source of Watergate fame. (The theater major next to him will of course be wondering what the title role in an old pornographic movie has to do with it.) Both students may share a romantic image that

Hollywood, and some journalists, have planted in their minds: A reporter in a trench coat slips into a dark alley and gets a sheaf of top secret papers from some unseen and never-to-be-revealed "source". It may have happened, but it's rare. Sources are not.

The professor continues to prod his students to name other sources, perhaps dropping hints, "What about a policeman at the scene of a crime? What about a doctor explaining the benefits of the latest vaccine? What about a witness to an accident or a grieving relative?" Gently, students are led to the obvious conclusion that anyone who provides information to a reporter is a "source". Suddenly, the image isn't nearly so romantic. We're all possible sources for something. When you pick up that phone call from a reporter, you're about to become one—and that may give you considerable leverage.

Taking Control

As a source, you have something a reporter wants. It may be the answer to a simple question. It may be access to your home or business. It may be an on-camera interview. Ultimately you decide what you will provide. A reporter has a whole array of tactics to use to persuade you to cooperate, tactics this book will cover. But by far the most common one is gentle persuasion. It's not very romantic, but it's usually the most effective. (You catch more flies with honey...) Reporters try to keep our sources happy, at least until we get what we want. We're trying to push your buttons, to persuade you to help us. But we have buttons that you can push too.

SPEAK UP!

If you want to influence the way a reporter tells a story, there's usually a catch: you have to agree to be part of it. To return to the example of violence in a school, lets say the intended "slant" is, *"Racial Violence disrupts Central High School..."* The reporter will want to talk to students who participated or who witnessed what happened. Such a story isn't flattering to the school. So the school officials often ban the cameras, and hope that lack of access will somehow prevent reporters from telling about it. That rarely works. A wiser response is to look for ways to make the story appear in a positive light, to change the "slant." Too often, schools don't see it that way.

A few years ago, I covered a student protest at a suburban high school, a protest that was clearly racist in tone. Some white student demonstrators were upset over an influx of minority students and a recent incident they described as a black-on-white attack. A little checking with school officials and police revealed a different account of what happened: While there had been a fight and one student was seriously injured, it was over a girl and those involved were *not* divided along racial lines. Yes, there was racial tension at the school, but it wasn't due to black on white assaults. Rather, it was due to the questionable perceptions of students like those who were protesting, an apparently small but vocal minority.

The demonstrators were eager to talk to the media. They even tipped us off in advance so we could get our cameras to their protest. However, as the facts became clear, I knew I needed to interview other witnesses and students who didn't share the protesters' opinions. What I found was that the school principal had made an announcement that morning, directing all students to refuse to talk to reporters. The protestors of course disregarded the request, while the students who were trying to do what was best for their school, obeyed.

The principal was saying in effect, "We don't want you to get the wrong impression of us, so we won't help you correct that impression." When I pointed out the lunacy of that approach, the principal finally agreed to be interviewed, but still denied me access to students. Fortunately, I was able to locate some student leaders off school grounds and persuade them to talk. With their help, I put together a much more balanced piece than would otherwise have been possible–a version that was more favorable to the school than the one I was first sent to tell. Still, even as I did the story, I had student after student ask me to leave. They felt that a few troublemakers were making the whole school look bad, but–dutifully following orders–they refused to do interviews to correct that impression.

It's a simple lesson that so many people never quite grasp when it comes to dealing with the media: *If you want to influence the way a story is told, you have to be willing to participate.* That doesn't always mean you have to do an interview. It does mean that you have to actively engage the reporter. The more you do, the more influence you'll have.

WHEN INTERESTS CONVERGE

The "big bad media" often deserves that perception, and contributes to it. We certainly have our failings. But there are also times when we can be very helpful, times when our interests and the interests of those we cover converge. Reporters and sources frequently work together out of common concerns, sometimes very effectively. The best example I know of is the case of one missing boy.

The Case of Jacob Wetterling

In October 1989, I was sent to a small town about an hour and a half from Minneapolis. There, the night before, a lone man had abducted an 11-year-old boy at gun point. The town was St. Joseph, Minnesota. The missing boy was Jacob Wetterling. Unfortunately, as this book is being written, he's still missing. But his story is a textbook case in how the interests of a family, a community, and the media can converge.

It wasn't the first time I'd reported on a missing child, and at first it felt like a routine assignment. I rotated onto the story with other reporters, and didn't even meet Jacob's family right away. Reporters on other shifts had interviewed them, and I knew it wasn't wise to knock on a distraught parent's door too often. When I did go to their door, I received an amazing welcome. They already knew who I was and had seen my work. They thanked me, and explained that the price of admission to their home–during what would become a long painful vigil–was a hug.

The Wetterlings realized, I think even before some of us did, that we were playing a role, a profoundly important role in whatever the outcome was to be. If they were ever going to get Jacob back, it would be because somebody who saw something or knew something came forward. They knew that the best way to bring that about was with maximum media attention.

Jacob's family made a courageous decision, to go completely public from the very beginning, and they used whatever ploys they could to attract attention and tug at people's emotions. They granted all requests for interviews. They invited us into their home, which was filled with relatives and friends around the clock. They released Jacob's favorite song, and it quickly became a media staple. The song was "Listen" by family music artist Red Grammer, and he came to visit and perform it.

The community also caught on to the strategy and began to orchestrate events—balloon launches, benefits, mass mailings, anything to attract cameras and reporters. A weekend rally drew a thousand people, singing and crying and praying for Jacob's return. It was a gathering so filled with emotion, that it left even many seasoned reporters red-eyed and in awe. The media interest was already high, but those activities made it possible for news organizations to keep the story alive much longer than any of us could have otherwise. The news —especially television— ultimately depends on events, something new to show people or tell them. If the latest facts each day had been simply, "Jacob is still missing," then coverage would soon have been equally minimal. As long as the family or the community was doing something, it was a story, even if the investigation had nothing new to tell.

I worked the story full-time for weeks, as did at least one reporter for every news organization in the state. I've never felt more useful in my life. My colleagues and I heard "thank you" many times a day—from investigators, from people in the community, and from the Wetterling family.

Jacob was the lead story on nearly every local newscast for nearly two weeks, and was soon drawing national media attention. The story stayed near the top of the news for months. Hundreds of volunteers joined members of the National Guard in the largest manhunt in Minnesota history. The search for clues soon stretched throughout the state and then the country, as the media publicized various descriptions of suspects and vehicles.

Investigators, from the local sheriff's department right up through the FBI welcomed the media. When authorities created a computer bank to track the thousands of leads that came in, they invited us to cover it. They held regular news conferences to announce any new developments. Over and over, they asked for help from the public, and they used the media to forward those requests.

The result was an unprecedented amount of publicity for such a case, especially when you consider how often children turn up missing these days. White ribbon bows became the designated symbol of "Jacob's Hope" and they appeared everywhere. One of our photographers who covered the story took to putting a bow on his camera. Later, when he was on assignment in Germany, someone asked, "Is that for the American boy missing from Minnesota?" The coverage was so intense that some people began to ask, "What's so special about Jacob Wetterling?" There are many good answers to that question, many things that made the case unique. But the publicity came partly because of a family's intense desire to find their boy, combined with the recognition that the media could help do that.

The Wetterlings realized that reporters were a tool they could use to help find their son, and they definitely used us. We knew exactly what they were up to, and willingly went along, because all they were asking us to do was our jobs. Over time reporters instinctively begin to look for ways to convince people that we're trying to help, that we share many of the same interests and concerns they do. Never has that been easier for me than with the Wetterlings. Among those of us who covered them, I'm not alone when I say I will always wish them well.

Adversaries?

Even negative stories are usually based on some level of mutual interest. The stories that on the surface look the most antagonistic are often the ones that required the greatest trust between reporters and newsmakers. For every story of abuse and fraud, for every villain painted by the media, there's at least one source who felt it was in his or her interest to assist the reporter–or the story could never be told. We get such stories not by "going after people" but by finding people willing to help us.

Just as the '92 Republican National Convention began, the *New York Times* printed a story alleging that the Bush Administration had concocted a plan to begin bombing Iraq–during the time of the convention. It was a strategy to pressure the still recalcitrant Iraqi leader Saddam Hussein into submission to the U.N.'s cease-fire terms following the Persian Gulf War. Presumably it would also boost Bush's image as a tough world leader, at a critical time in his re-election campaign. The article explained a scenario in which United Nations arms inspection teams would demand to see a particular Iraqi building or facility. If Hussein refused, as he had previously, U.S. planes would then attack that building. The same routine would then be repeated at another site and so forth. According to the story, the plan had the approval of our allies and the U.N.

President Bush vehemently denied that there was such a plan, or that he had the cynical political motives that the alleged timing of the plan implied. To many convention delegates, the story became yet another example of "liberal media bias"–proof that we were out to discredit Bush, whose denial they accepted. One delegate, who was obviously angry about the article, asked me, "How in the world does a reporter get a story like that?"

I assured him that I had no way of knowing how this particular story surfaced, and no way of personally confirming that the story was true. Then I explained that all that the *Times* reporter would have needed was a couple of good sources. Such sources might have been eager to tell what they knew, even to the point of calling a trusted reporter.

A plan of the type described would have to be discussed with a fairly large number of people. First, within the administration and the military, then with our allies, with the U.N. and so forth. Such a plan would have been certain to set off alarms in some of those circles. It would have raised questions about the safety of U.N. inspection teams, just for starters. The surest way to prevent such a plan from being carried out, is to "leak" it to some reporter—a reporter who can be counted on not to betray the source. Like the chain that's only as strong as its weakest link, any one of dozens of people could have broken the silence.

To be sure, few reporters would take such a tip at face value. The source would need to be a reliable one, and provide information which could somehow be confirmed. The point is that a reporter's antagonism doesn't break stories like that. Trusting relationships between us and our sources do. A good reporter knows that and places a high value on such relationships. One of the keys to working with a reporter—and becoming an ally instead of a target—is to *Make sure you're someone who can be trusted.*

CHAPTER TWO:

THE BASICS

When I was in graduate school trying to learn the skills of my trade, I was fortunate to learn most of them from professionals who worked in television or other media. One of my favorite instructors was one of the most experienced journalists I've ever known, a news veteran named Walt Bodine. Walt has spent virtually his entire career in my home town of Kansas City. He's never had much fame outside that part of the Midwest, and to my knowledge never sought it. But he's worked in radio and in television news since its infancy. He's been a reporter, a talk-show host, a news director, a commentator, a newspaper columnist and, thankfully for me, an instructor of aspiring journalists.

It was Walt's chore to try to teach me how to write for television and radio, and it was surely one of his greatest challenges. I remember him lecturing us on the need to always be specific in what we wrote, so his Great Rule Number One was: "Generalities are Bullshit." (–Except this one.) It was one of his "Three Great Rules" for broadcast writing. I won't take the time to explain the other two here. You don't need to know them unless you plan to be a reporter. But I do have some suggestions for you, should you ever have to face one of us. So I've decided to borrow Walt's approach and offer you my "Three Great Rules" for *handling* a reporter.

Walt's rules were those things he considered the most crucial for us to know. He said that if we learned nothing else from his class, to please remember those few simple precepts. My "Three Great Rules" are equally crucial. They're not tactics or strategies; they're bedrock principles that should underlie everything else you do when you're dealing with the media. So just as he told us, let me tell you: If you learn nothing else from this book, remember these few basic guidelines.

GREAT RULE # 1: *ASSUME YOU'RE ALWAYS ON THE RECORD.*

This is a public relations consultant's favorite rule. It's safest. It leaves the least to chance. It doesn't leave you at the mercy of the reporter's good will. And it doesn't require a particularly high skill level by whoever's getting the advice. The point is simple: When you're talking to a reporter, *Don't say anything you don't want everybody to hear.* There are exceptions to this rule. Anonymous sources and "off the record" conversations have their place, but those are special arrangements that a reporter and source agree to *in advance.* Those sorts of restrictions—and the risks that come with them—are something I'll explain in a later chapter.

There are some very famous instances of people getting into trouble for breaking this rule. Despite the publicity they get, new ones keep surfacing. President Nixon's Agriculture Secretary, Earl Butz, was forced to resign from his cabinet post after telling a very off-color racial joke casually on a plane. The joke doesn't bear repeating here, but the reporter who heard it thought it did at the time. Jimmy the Greek was let go by CBS Sports, after making the observation that blacks were more gifted athletes than whites because of selective breeding by slave owners. Andy Rooney was suspended from his job on *60 minutes*, after he was quoted making some disparaging remarks about homosexuals. The issue here isn't political correctness. It's discretion. These are professionals, who should be well aware of the risks involved in making those kinds of statements. Still, they had to learn the hard way.

Don't drive off the same cliff. You don't have to be a public figure to suffer serious consequences from an ill-conceived remark. It may not matter whether everyone hears you on the news, only that one particular person hears you, such as your employer, a client or a close friend. Once you've said it to a reporter, you can't take it back.

Broadcast Alert:

A special caution applies when you're talking to a broadcast reporter. For some reason people tend to think that since television reporters use cameras, we can't see or hear without one. They sometimes assume the same thing about a radio reporter who doesn't have a tape recorder rolling. Certainly a broadcast reporter prefers to have statements on tape, but we can also quote you. We're less likely to use what you say when the tape isn't rolling, but we will if we think it's good enough. We'll simply attribute it to you, just as a print reporter would.

GREAT RULE # 2: *BE HONEST.*

I shouldn't have to say this, but I do. I realize there are times when you can't be completely candid. I know it's more than a little awkward admitting to a reporter that your company is about to lay people off when you haven't told your employees yet. I know investigators don't reveal every detail about a crime. Families have a right to keep some things private. But you can almost always avoid outright lies.

Keep in mind that you're not just lying to some reporter whom you may hardly know. You're lying to everyone who sees that reporter's story. Breaking a trust between yourself and a journalist can be dangerous enough. But you're also breaking a trust between everyone else who may hear or read it. Your credibility is an easy thing to lose.

Prevaricate, Maybe; But Lie? Never.

Being caught in a deliberate falsehood can be an ugly sight. I've seen people come off looking very foolish when they've tried to lie their way out of a situation. I've seen it happen to Fortune 500 corporations, like Control Data. There was a time when Control Data was one of the towering giants of the computer industry, one of its greatest success stories. Then, in the mid '80s, when hard times hit the computer business, Control Data was one of the companies hit hardest.

Before the problems had become obvious to everyone, a reporter in our news room learned from a very reliable source that massive layoffs were imminent. The company flatly denied it. We believed that the information we had was good, so we went with the story anyway, and the company then attacked us–questioning our credibility. Control Data Management even sent a letter to all its employees, accusing us of being irresponsible and sensationalizing the story.

Within weeks the layoffs began. In less than a year everything our story had predicted had come true. Here was a company whose management must have known what was going to happen, and chose to dispute it. There are better ways to handle such situations.

What else could the company have done? One alternative would have been to issue a simple statement, perhaps something like this:

"Our industry is in a downturn (*which was already becoming known*) so we are reviewing our staffing situation–as are other computer companies. But no decisions have been made."

If that would still have been a lie, it certainly was a much smaller one. It's the kind of statement that says everything and therefore says almost nothing. At that point you can decline to discuss details, either because it's too sensitive or because, as you said, "No decisions have been made."

Would that have satisfied the reporter? Probably not. But it would have come closer than stonewalling on the story, and you haven't said anything that can be held against you later.

Why lie at all? What's the harm in being completely candid with everyone involved?

Would it alarm employees and investors? It might. But no more so than the story did anyway, and when you have to take the necessary actions, you can honestly say you've tried to be up front with those people.

Isn't it better to notify employees directly first? Of course, but it may be too late for that. If that courtesy is your only concern, call them together or memo them today and tell them before the story appears. I've seen it done.

The deception ultimately undermined the company's credibility with the public and with its employees. At first, my news room was the target of great anger. Our switchboard lit up with hundreds of calls from people who preferred to believe the company rather than us. But that shifting of blame was only temporary. Some months later, I was at Control Data on another story. As I was being escorted around, I noticed a television in an employee lounge and joked that it surely wasn't tuned to my station. The employee with me quietly said, "Are you kidding? We all watch you guys. It's the only way we can find out what's really going on around here."

(Postscript: Control Data is now a completely reorganized renamed company, and has shown remarkable improvement in many areas, including its media relations.)

Don't Say More Than You Know to be True.

This can be a much more insidious kind of dishonesty. It's not quite the same as a lie, but it can be just as damaging. It's a trap that's easy to fall into even with the best of intentions. When you're on the defensive, it's especially easy to find yourself asserting facts you don't really know for sure. Reporters pride themselves on being able to spot such lapses. It's a skill we hone on some politicians, who can be quite adept at stating things they can't back up, hoping no one will notice the gaps in their logic.

When I was reporting for WTVH-TV in Syracuse, New York, there was a horrific elevator accident in a dormitory at Syracuse University. At first all we knew was that rescue crews found a young student's body in the bottom of an elevator shaft. It would be a week before reporters with the Syracuse newspaper pieced together a scenario in which an elevator repairman had overridden all the safety devices, using controls at the top of the building. He had started the elevator just as the young man was trying to get off, many floors below. The student was pinned in the closing elevator doors, and crushed to death as the car rose.

Immediately after the accident, the university restricted all media from the building, and for days officials released only the most minimal information. Finally, the president of S.U. held a news conference. Before a room filled with cameras and reporters, he read a carefully prepared statement. He expressed the university's regrets. He told us that no cause for the accident had been determined yet, and an investigation was still underway. Then he made some assertions that his other remarks clearly didn't support. He told us that there was no evidence that the university was responsible, and that no one had found any negligence or direct involvment by university employees. As he read on, he sounded like someone who was fending off potential lawsuits, before he could even tell us what happened! I'm sure that wasn't the perception he intended but it was one he created. It's tough enough to prove a negative, but he was trying to do it without any alternative explanation.

By the time he finished, we were not sympathetic. Reporters began to ask questions, trying to get more information, and not having success. After waiting so long for so little, our reaction was hostility. Finally, more than a little exasperated, I asked him,

"Do you know what caused this to happen?"

"No," he answered, as I knew he would.

"Then how can you stand there and tell us this is just some freak accident?" (And you already know who's *not* responsible?)

What followed was an incredibly long silence. We timed it later on tape and he didn't speak for almost 30 seconds. Finally he stammered for a few moments and then answered, very tentatively,

"I'm referring...to it...as an accident...because...at this time...that is what...we believe it...to be."

I confess I felt very smug at that moment. It was one of those delightful times in a reporter's career when you know you have utterly nailed someone–someone who I honestly felt deserved it. One of my competitors quietly complimented me before we'd even finished the news conference. The story I aired included my question–and the entire pause–as well as the president's answer. I had no qualms about letting my viewers see his obvious discomfort.

You don't always have to know everything. There are times when it's appropriate to give an expert opinion that goes beyond proven facts. A police officer at the scene of a crime, may describe what appears to have happened. A firefighter may say arson is the suspected cause of a fire. An executive may offer an honest assessment of his business. What will get you into trouble is drawing unqualified conclusions that you can't support.

GREAT RULE # 3: *KNOW WHAT YOU CAN'T SAY.*

This may be a free country, but there are certain things you should *never* say to a reporter–because it's against the law. Libel and slander are things for which either a source or a reporter can be sued. Anything derogatory that you say about another person is possible grounds for such a lawsuit, if it's untrue. If it's true, you should be okay. As lawyers sometimes say about such cases, "Truth is the ultimate defense." But you still need to be careful. The catch is: Can you prove it's true? If you can't, you may not want to say it.

How you phrase something can make a big difference. When you express an opinion such as, "I don't feel that he can be trusted," you're making a subjective statement that is neither true nor false. It would be very difficult for anyone to prove that's slander. On the other hand, if you say, "He lied to me," then you've asserted something that could later be proven to be untrue, which is possible grounds for a lawsuit. You can safely call someone a "jerk" if you want. That's an opinion. But don't call them a "child abuser"–unless you can back it up.

The reporter has a responsibility not to repeat libelous or slanderous statements. If anyone's likely to be sued, it's probably the media. But we have more protection than you do. It's called The First Amendment. The courts have ruled that someone bringing such a lawsuit against a reporter must prove that there was negligence. If the person who's suing is famous or well known, the standard is even higher. A public figure must prove that the reporter had "malicious intent" or "reckless disregard for the truth". Those are tough requirements designed to protect the freedom of the press. They don't necessarily protect you if you've deliberately deceived a reporter or withheld important information.

I recently discovered to my amazement that Minnesota has a law on the books, making it a criminal offense to give false statements to a reporter. I don't know when it's ever been enforced, or how many other states have similar statutes, but it's something to keep in mind.

Some other legal restrictions are very specific. Federal laws control what someone can say publicly about securities transactions. State and federal privacy laws prohibit anyone from disclosing all sorts of confidential records. In most states, it's against the law for a psychiatric hospital to reveal who any of its patients are without the patient's permission. There are privacy restrictions on some police and court records–particularly involving children. Other privacy laws cover everything from personnel and credit files to school records. Private companies have a right to keep certain types of proprietary secrets, and can sue someone who reveals them. If you have access to any of these types of information, you probably already know more about what you can or can't do with them than I do. Any questions you have, you should probably direct to a good attorney. The penalties can be serious.

When it comes to releasing confidential data, not all reporters know what's legal and what's not, but again we're not always as much at risk as you are. The courts have repeatedly ruled against "prior restraint" on the media, so laws designed to restrict information are generally directed at sources. That means in some instances a reporter may have the legal right to use information that it may be illegal for you to disclose. You're the one who's breaking the law. Be careful.

* * *

All three Great Rules have one thing in common: *They're all things that you can control.* You decide what to say to a reporter, and whether to be truthful. You know whether you can back up your assertions and you can readily find out what information you can or can't legally reveal.

When you're dealing with the news media, many things are controlled by the reporter, while your challenge is to try to wield some influence. But no reporter can force you to lie or criticize. The ability to choose what you say is one very important power that you always retain.

CHAPTER THREE:
TO TALK
OR
NOT TO TALK

The ability to get the media's attention is an art. Knowing that art is a profession, and often a very lucrative one. It's called public relations or media relations. Corporations, public officials, and political advocacy groups are just a few examples of newsmakers who often set out to "make news" and then do it. But by far the majority of people in the news each day got there without any planning on their part. They didn't call a reporter. A reporter called them. They simply respond, and how they respond often has a lot to do with how we tell their story.

I'm continually amazed at the people who talk to me, sometimes sharing their most intimate secrets in ways I doubt I would if I were the one being questioned. At times I'm just as amazed at the people who refuse to answer even the most harmless question. Whatever the person's decision, it's frequently based on an at-best-vague understanding of why I'm asking for something, or what I will do with it once I get it.

As a journalist, it would certainly be easier for me if I could persuade everyone to talk to me, no matter what the circumstances. The reality is people don't always talk to reporters. There are sometimes good reasons not to—although I have colleagues who think it's heresy for me to say so. Only you can decide when you will talk, what you will say and under what circumstances. But before you decide, there are some things it's helpful to know—about the story, about the reporter, and about yourself.

WHY SHOULD YOU TALK?

I firmly believe that in most situations it's best to answer a reporter's questions. (I know, that's easy for me to say.) It can be frightening to hand yourself over to a stranger who has the power to make you look foolish, or worse, if the reporter wants. Putting our faith in the media, is not something most of us do lightly. How far you go depends partly on your personality. In my experience, the people who are often the least cooperative are people accustomed to being in control. Judges and business executives are often difficult to persuade to talk, even though they are well-educated and articulate people who should be the most skilled at handling such situations. What they don't realize is that *By talking, you are increasing your control over the situation.* Until you agree to talk, you have virtually no influence over the story. If you're willing to cooperate, at least in some way, you give yourself three advantages you don't otherwise have. You have the power to **negotiate,** to **educate** and to **communicate**.

Negotiate

As I explained in the first chapter, the reporter wants something from you. Perhaps it's access to your home or business, an interview with you, or just some information. If you're willing to give whatever that is, you may be able to get something from the reporter in return. That may be information about the intent of the story, and the assurance that the reporter will handle the story a certain way. The reporter isn't going to give you editorial control, but you have every right to ask what the reporter's intentions are–and the right to try to change those intentions when you disagree.

No reporter ever calls and just says, "I want to talk to you, at this time and this place. Be there." We begin with some explanation of what the story is and why we need you to be part of it. We know that if we want information, we must be willing to give some. So we anticipate some of the questions we would expect you to ask. Sometimes we will make concessions to win your cooperation. By calling you, a reporter is in effect giving you the power to influence the story. Use it. Ask questions. Make requests.

The things that reporters and sources negotiate are virtually limitless. They range from whether we will identify the source, to the scope of the questions we ask, to what information we will or won't include in the piece. How flexible the reporter will be, or how flexible you should be, depends on the circumstances. It's rarely possible for either of you to dictate terms without considering how the other will react.

Educate

If you ask the right questions, you should be able to determine what the story is to be. Or, you'll discover that the reporter doesn't intend for you to know. Either way you have some useful information. If you like the approach being taken, fine, do the story. If you disagree, don't hang up. That's not likely to make the story go away. Instead, try to persuade the reporter to do the story more to your liking. That usually means *educating* the reporter.

The opportunity to educate the reporter is your most powerful weapon. You almost certainly know more about your business, family or whatever than we do. If you think the reporter's approach is unfair or insensitive, say so. Offer whatever facts you can to bolster your case. The more information you're willing to provide, the stronger your case will be.

Even when we take you by surprise—perhaps an employee of yours is accused of committing a crime and the reporter is the first to tell you about it—don't refuse to talk. Instead, offer to get back to the reporter after you've had a chance to check out the facts for yourself.

The important thing is to keep an open dialogue. As long as you have the reporter's ear, you have an opportunity to change his or her mind and influence the story. Reporters consider it part of our professional responsibility to tell all sides. One of the most effective tactics you can use is to "help" us be thorough.

Communicate

There's one other benefit of engaging a reporter that's often overlooked. *It's a way to communicate with your "stakeholders"*. When you appear in the news, you're of course not just talking to a reporter, and you're not just talking to the public as a whole. You're also talking to other specific individuals who have a stake in your actions. Who they are will depend on the circumstances. To an employer, it may be employees; to an entrepreneur, investors; to a professional, clients. If you're a politician, you're talking to your constituents; police talk to the citizenry; and we're all talking to our neighbors and families.

A news report does something that no internal memo or letter can ever do. It conveys the message that, "I'm willing to face public scrutiny, to be fully on the record with everyone." You may not care a whit what some reporter thinks of you, but you probably care what your employees or bosses think. You can bet they'll be watching. You can defend them, ignore them, or lie to them, through a news report. You can make your concerns and priorities clear to the people who most need to know where you're coming from, or you can leave them uncertain. You can reassure your colleagues that you're being totally above board, or you can make statements "for public consumption" that completely contradict things you've said privately. It's up to you.

The media is a powerful instrument that all too often goes unused. Police have a distrust of reporters that is legendary. Many departments avoid dealing with us whenever possible. Those investigators who use us—and I do mean *use*—know how helpful we can be. The city of St. Paul, where I do much of my work, has one of the more enlightened departments I've found. The head of homicide is a lieutenant named Joe Corcoran. Joe goes to the media frequently, and he's the first to say that he does it because it solves crimes. He can cite case after case, where publicity has generated phone calls, and created leads that led to arrests. He takes many of those calls himself, because people ask for him after seeing him on the news. It's just one of many reasons why St. Paul police are in the habit of clearing more than 90% of the city's homicides.

A little publicity can save considerable work, even when it doesn't lead to arrests. When several parents witnessed a man photographing children on their way to school, one of the mothers contacted my news room. She and other parents first notified the school and police. Then she called us to be sure to alert everyone in the area to the possible danger. She feared that school officials and police wouldn't issue such an alert—and she was right. The school had no intention of contacting the media, even though it was the second time someone had witnessed the same suspicious activity. The district had a policy of sending fliers home to warn parents of its students about such incidents, but it gave no notice to the rest of the community. It's a policy typical of school districts, who tend to be at least as worried about their image as they are about student safety.

I did a story on the sighting and the concern it created among parents. After it aired, we received a call from an attorney. She explained that the man seen taking pictures was an insurance adjuster, who she had sent to photograph an intersection near the school as part of an accident investigation. The fact that children had been there was incidental, and had obviously led to a serious misunderstanding. After talking to the photographer, witnesses and police, we ran an update explaining what had happened.

Police were thrilled that we saved them all the trouble of trying to track down someone who had apparently committed no crime anyway. Investigators were planning to put an undercover officer near the school, to try to catch him. The mother who talked to me felt a little embarrassed about the fuss she had made, until I explained to her how much she had helped. If she hadn't come forward, police would still be looking for someone who had done nothing wrong. The publicity was what put the matter to rest.

It's popular to talk about corporate culture these days. Organizations have personalities that determine not only how they behave internally, but how they react to the outside community–including the media. Lt. Corcoran wouldn't be so cooperative without the blessing of the chief. The way you respond to the media is itself an indicator of what kind of person you are, or the kind of organization of which you're a part.

Talking to a reporter carries risks, but it also conveys a sense of openness. Refusing to talk does just the opposite, and it tends to reinforce that behavior among other members of a business or agency. If you have uncomfortable secrets to keep, stonewall reporters and severely penalize anyone who breaks the code of silence. The government, the military and the Mafia have all been doing that for years. So have many major corporations. If you feel your actions are honorable, defend them, and you'll be encouraging others to do the same.

PRIVACY: WHAT'S YOUR THRESHOLD?

Even before you begin asking a reporter questions about a story, there's one you need to ask yourself. It's a deceptively simple one;

"How much do I want to tell *everyone*?"

Your answer probably changes depending on the topic. Most of us feel more comfortable talking about the weather than we do about our sex lives. But we all know someone who loves to brag about sexual exploits. And I once had a weather person get very upset with me for joking on the air about an incorrect forecast. We each have our set of standards, and we tend to take offense when other people–such as reporters–don't share our standards. You have to decide what your "threshold" is.

A "Stark" Contrast

As the U.S.S. Stark was cruising the Persian Gulf in the spring of 1987, the ship was hit by an Exocet missile fired by an Iraqi fighter. The Iran-Iraq War had suddenly resulted in U.S. casualties. News organizations throughout the country scrambled to find out what servicemen and women were aboard and whether they had relatives in our respective cities. It didn't take us long to find the family of 20-year-old Signalman, Christopher Ryden. Crews from four television stations, two newspapers and local radio, all converged on the Ryden home to cover an anguishing vigil that would last for days. While the Rydens waited for word on whether Christopher had survived, each television station aired live reports from the Ryden living room. Ryden's parents and other family members found themselves doing interview after interview and even had cameras videotaping them as they took phone calls.

Finally, word came that Christopher was all right, and the media blitz ended. A week or so later, a letter to the editor appeared in the Minneapolis newspaper criticizing the media. The irate writer asked,

> "...When ordinary families are thrust into the spotlight through no fault of their own, must they become easy prey for the media in hot pursuit of an interview?...Can any media intrusion be justified in the name of news?..."

Those are troubling questions we reporters sometimes ask ourselves, and it wasn't long until someone responded. Soon another letter to the editor appeared, one written by Christopher's uncle. He said he was responding to the previous letter and he wanted to *thank* the news media, saying,

> "...We did not become 'prey' for the news media, but rather we welcomed them into our homes and office because they showed a genuine sympathy and total respect for the feelings of our family. At no time were they ever abusive, demanding or rude... I have never seen people more concerned with propriety than the camera crews and reporters who were in the living room of my brother's house. They were someone to talk with, laugh with and cry with during these difficult hours..."

Two dramatically different reactions to the same situation, and both strongly felt. We all have different thresholds for what we consider to be an invasion of our privacy. Each of us has different ways of handling stress. For some, being able to share our worries or our grief is therapeutic; it's an important emotional release. For others it's an offensive intrusion. Neither approach is inherently right or wrong. Reactions often vary within a single family. One relative may be much more willing and able to deal with the media than another.

As for pressure from reporters, most of us realize that in sensitive situations, a soft-sell is usually the most effective. Reporters who are pushy frequently end up on the outside looking in.

You need to decide what's best for you and your family or business. That means asking yourself questions you may never have thought about. You may feel strongly that you do not want live cameras in your living room or office, but how do you feel about doing a videotaped interview? What about the print reporter who only carries a notepad? What if she brings along a still photographer? What do you do when you've agreed to speak to one reporter and another one calls? Like many things about dealing with reporters, there's usually no simple "Yes" or "No" answer. It's a question of degree.

COMFORT VS. CONSEQUENCES

Deciding what to do would be easy if the only thing that mattered was how you felt. But finding your comfort level is only half of the equation. You also need to have some idea how the reporter will react to your decision, and what may happen next. To determine those things, there are questions you should ask. You want to try to find out what the reporter will do when you say, "Yes," or, "No." How will your decision affect the story that will result? Will it be more or less favorable to you? What follows are some of the crucial questions you need answered.

What's the Story?

The first thing you need to know when a reporter calls is, "Why am I being contacted?" In other words, "What's the story and how does it involve me?" If the answer isn't obvious, ask, but most of the time that's the first thing the reporter will tell you. Listen carefully. Don't let the reporter get away with something like, "I'm doing a story on child care." That gives you the topic, but you still don't know the angle. Is it a story about the need for child care, or is it about inadequate regulation of child care centers? Were you called because the reporter wants to use pictures of your preschooler and talk to you about the hassles of finding a nanny? Were you called because you're an expert on early childhood development? Or were you called because you run a child care center that is being investigated for alleged abuse? Obviously you want to know whether the reporter intends to treat you favorably or unfavorably. You want to know whether you need to prepare to defend yourself, or if you're just being used as an illustration of some problem or concern.

It's always easier to talk when the story is favorable, but it may be crucial that you talk when you're on the defensive. It's your opportunity to make your case.

Where Did the Story Come From?

How did the reporter find out about the story, or about me? Who else has been interviewed, or will be? What have other people already said? The answers to those questions will give you some idea what the reporter already knows and help you gauge the reporter's motives and level of expertise. If the story is about allegations of improper business practices by you, did the reporter hear about them from the Better Business Bureau or your competitor across the street? If the call is about the latest oncology research, whose study is it? Will the reporter even understand your answers without some careful explaining?

If a confidential source was used to locate you or to find the information you're being asked about, the reporter probably won't reveal it to you. Still it doesn't hurt to ask. You may get a partial answer, and in any case you may get a sense of how the reporter is handling the story. If the reporter isn't forthcoming, should you be?

You may also want to know if the reporter seems to already have enough material to do the story without your help, or if this is some sort of "fishing expedition". In short, learning where the reporter has been, will usually give you some idea where the story is headed. That should give you clues to whether you need to try to redirect the story, and how to do that.

Am I "Critical?"

You need to know whether you're an essential element in the story that the reporter wants to tell. Is the story about you, or your family or business, or about something you did? Is it based on information only you can give? Or are there other people the reporter could call instead, someone else who could serve as an illustration?

Your being critical to a story can be both a blessing and a curse. It means the reporter may put considerable pressure on you to cooperate. You'll get the hard sell, maybe veiled threats if you're being targeted for something. A central role can also give you some added leverage. You may be able to say, "Yes, I'll do what you want, if..." Even when you're in retreat, there may still be some room to maneuver. An offer to grant an interview can sometimes win other concessions, perhaps limiting the scope of the questions to be asked, or a promise not to disclose your whereabouts.

I once went to interview a man who had been shot in the chest, as he was taking out the trash in his own back yard. His first words to me were, "No names, no faces, no address." Without hesitating, I agreed. He was central to the story. An interview with him was the difference between a compelling human interest tale, and one more crime statistic. Who's involved and exactly where it happened are normally the first things mentioned in a brief crime story. But I was glad to trade a few impersonal facts for an interview with the victim, even if I had to hide his identity. By talking, he was able to ensure that the story contained *less* information than if he had refused to speak to me.

When the reporter is just looking for an illustration, the pressure on you may not be so great. If you won't do it, perhaps someone else will, so you can afford to be more conservative. Whether you're flattered to be chosen, or uncomfortable with the request will of course depend on the story. If you don't want a camera present during your vasectomy, politely say so.

If you're not critical to the story, you can decline to participate, with little risk that your name will ever come up at all. When a reporter is looking for someone willing to talk about using illegal drugs, you can bet more than one person gets a call before the reporter finds someone willing to discuss it publicly. The story doesn't list those people who turned down the request. On the other hand, if the story is that you've been charged with illegal drug use, you're almost certain to be named, whether or not the reporter can even reach you. The reporter may want to assure those who see the story that every attempt was made to reach you. So the story will include a statement like, "So-and-so refused to talk to us." If you're that person, you have to decide whether that sounds better or worse than whatever you might have to say.

Is it "Breaking News" or "Enterprise"?

You probably want to know whether you're going to be dealing with just one reporter or many. You might feel up to doing one interview about your missing daughter, but can you handle two—or twenty?

One simple test to determine the potential interest in a story is to ask yourself (or the reporter), "Is this story tied to some particular event that just happened or is about to?" Has there been an accident? Is there an investigation underway? Has my company been fined for something? If the answer is, "Yes," then it's what reporters call, "breaking news". That can be anything from a plane crash, to a crime, to a public protest scheduled for that day.

If it's a breaking story, then you probably will hear from more than one reporter–even if it's a story based on something that's not public yet. If one reporter can find out about it, others probably can too. That means whatever you say, you should be prepared to repeat, perhaps many times. Maybe you want to do a series of interviews, or call a news conference. (More on that later.)

The other kind of story is what reporters call an "enterprise" piece. This includes investigative stories. On this kind of story, a reporter takes a topic or an idea or maybe a tip and checks into it. It might be a complex story on organized crime that the reporter has been looking into for months. Or it might be nothing more than a request to ride along on a farmer's combine for an hour and ask how the harvest is going. Since the story isn't tied to any particular event, it's not as likely that any other reporter is doing the same piece–although that does happen.

* * *

Armed with the information you have now collected, you can decide whether you want to cooperate or not. If you say, "No," the reporter may say, "Thank you," and that will be the end of it. If you say, "Yes," you may do a 10 minute interview, get the 15 minutes of fame that Andy Warhol promised each of us, and never see the reporter again. I'm sure you already realize that it often isn't that simple. You may just be getting started.

CHAPTER FOUR:

WHEN YOU WANT
TO TALK

Have I pursuaded you to talk yet? If I have, I've done it using the same arguments you're likely to hear when some reporter calls. A reporter who can't convince people to speak isn't worth much, so that's one of the first skills we develop (or we give up and look for more honorable work). Convincing *you* has no doubt been easier than with some sources. If you were determined never to talk to a reporter, you wouldn't be reading this book, or at least not this chapter.

Reporters talk about interviews as though they're trophies or little gifts. We say things like, "I got an interview from..." or, "She gave me some great 'quotes'." The arrangements can vary from quite simple, to staggering in their complexity. At one extreme, a reporter makes a simple phone call, to confirm one fact. Or a lone photographer pushes a microphone at Christmas shoppers to find out how much they're spending. At the other extreme are elaborate preparations, to accommodate thousands of cameras and journalists at a national political convention. Whatever the circumstances, the source almost certainly has something to say about it. It's an opportunity for you to exert some control–sometimes considerable control.

THE BRIAN COYLE STORY

Minneapolis City Council Member Brian Coyle had known for six years that he carried the AIDS virus, when he decided to go public with it. For an elected official to keep his AIDS status secret for so long had been no small feat–especially for one who was openly gay. But that achievement pales in comparison to the way he orchestrated how the media told his story, and how he kept it a secret for months after he first revealed it to a reporter. Even when a second reporter learned of Coyle's HIV status, Coyle was able to bring him into a complex arrangement that determined when and how the story appeared.

Coyle knew two things: He knew his story was a potential political and personal bombshell, which could blow up in his face if not handled properly. He also knew from years of experience with the media, how to handle reporters. What he wanted was a positive story about his personal struggle with the disease. He wanted to limit any political or personal damage to himself. And he wanted to send a message of hope for others with AIDS.

He began by revealing his HIV status to free-lance journalist David Carr. *Minnesota Monthly*, a local magazine, eagerly agreed to publish the story, and Carr arranged to do a series of interviews. By offering the story exclusively to the magazine and Carr, Coyle got assurances that the story would be handled tastefully, and not be sensationalized. Coyle would be able to prepare himself for the response from the public and his colleagues, because he would know months ahead when the story would appear.

The plan came dangerously close to failing. Three months later–and still before the story was published–a television reporter called and asked for a meeting with Coyle. Through other sources, Investigative Reporter Joel Grover had learned of Coyle's HIV status, and confronted him with it.

Someone else might have "stonewalled" the second reporter. Coyle could have denied the truth, hoping to hold together the original deal, even though it was obviously coming apart. Instead, he did something much shrewder. He admitted the truth and cut a second deal. The terms were similar: assurances from Grover that he would do a sensitive and positive story, in exchange for a *"Broadcast* exclusive". With this second arrangement Coyle effectively gained control of his story in a second medium, television as well as print. At the same time he took a reporter who could have undone all of Coyle's carefully laid plans, and gave that reporter a strong motive to protect his secret.

For weeks, Carr and Grover each spent many hours with Coyle, following him through his daily routine. By now the story also involved a camera. So the agreed ruse was that Grover was working on a story about gay public figures.

Through complex negotiations, Coyle, the magazine and KSTP television arranged for the story to break in a way that was to everyone's advantage. First, Coyle's many friends and colleagues received a letter from him, explaining his HIV status. That night KSTP broke the story, and the first of a three-part in-depth series began on its 10 o'clock news. The next morning, the May '91 issue of *Minnesota Monthly* began arriving in subscribers' mailboxes. KSTP scooped all its competitors–including my news room–and that coverage had the effect of promoting interest in the magazine article. Once the story was out, Coyle called a news conference. It was one for which he'd had plenty of time to prepare.

Coyle avoided the media frenzy that could so easily have erupted from an unplanned disclosure. He wasn't put in the unflattering position of "confirming rumors" or "refusing to comment". No other news organization could match the quality and depth of coverage given by the reporters in whom Coyle had confided. Their work set a standard, so as other reporters played catch-up, there was little temptation to hype it, or to in any way "go after" Coyle. The tone had been set, and it was exactly the tone he wanted. What he achieved was, in the words of David Carr, "Consummate media manipulation."

In a sense, Coyle managed to write his own obituary. Within just a few months, he died of complications related to AIDS.

What Coyle did was fraught with risks. His whole plan could have unraveled at any time. It's not an approach I would recommend to the unskilled or faint hearted. But it shows just how effectively you can control the media if you know how. This chapter is about how to maintain influence over a story as it unfolds. Brian Coyle wasn't trying to create news. He wasn't trying to pitch a story. (He didn't have to.) He was *reacting* to the inevitable media interest, but he was reacting *proactively*–and so should you.

MAKING ARRANGEMENTS–
WHAT TO EXPECT

The reporter will always ask to do things some particular way. I've never met an accomplished reporter who didn't like to be in control of the situation. If it's not a basic personality trait, it's something we quickly acquire to cope with the demands of our profession. It usually makes sense to do whatever a reasonable reporter asks. After all, who knows better how to put a story together? However there are times when you can orchestrate things, and probably should. At the very least, you should ask some important questions.

When There's One Reporter

It's usually simplest to deal with just one reporter. So let's take that case first. That means you've concluded that this is an "enterprise" story (chapter 3). Remember, the reporter wants something from you, so you have some leverage to use to make sure you're comfortable. If you don't approve of some of the arrangements, say so and propose an alternative you like.

What Will You Be Asked?

Specifically, what information does the reporter want to get from you? By now you should already know why one of us called, but is there any information you may need to get before the interview? A radio or print reporter will often want to interview you immediately, right there on the phone. That may be easiest for both of you, but if you need more time to prepare, say so. In television we will usually be asking to meet with you to talk on camera. Are there things you want time to think about in advance?

Will the reporter expect you to know your company's policy on sexual harassment? Can you quote the latest findings in the research that the reporter wants to discuss? Maybe all the reporter wants is your impression of something–the taxes you pay, crime in your neighborhood, or the job the President is doing. You probably still want a little warning to think about what your impressions are.

Don't ask for a list of questions. Most reporters don't make up a written list in advance, and when we do, we prefer not to give it to you. It's usually not a matter of any intended deception. It's just that a good interview flows according to the way you answer questions and the way the reporter follows up those answers. When someone receives the questions in advance, the temptation is to over-prepare and give "canned" answers. The result is usually not very useful to the reporter and may not be flattering to you, because it doesn't look natural. It's like someone "reading" a speech instead of delivering it. You get the feeling they're not really talking to you. That's not the best impression to leave.

What's the Deadline?

You need to know how soon the reporter wants to talk to you. Deadlines can range from "within the hour" for a radio reporter or someone working for the Associated Press, to literally months for a magazine article. For television and newspapers the answer will usually be, "Today, and the sooner the better." Does that fit your schedule? Are you willing to change your schedule to accommodate the reporter? If the topic is sensitive or complex, you may need some time to prepare. You may need to call a baby sitter. You may need to go get the car-with-the-faulty-transmission that the reporter wants to see.

Knowing the deadline tells you something about the type of story that the reporter intends to do. A story with a "today" deadline, is probably about something tied to today's events. It may be a story that we're likely to tell, with or without your cooperation. A story with a less urgent deadline is typically more in-depth or investigative. If the reporter doesn't intend to finish the story today, then it may be reasonable for you to take more time to prepare.

If the deadline seems inconsistent with the type of story, then you should expect an explanation. When a reporter tells you the story will appear next week, but the interview with you *must* be today, be sure the urgency is justified. Don't let it be an excuse to catch you off balance.

If the deadline is just hours away, obviously time is at a premium, for the reporter and for you. You'll want to prepare yourself quickly, to allow the reporter maximum time to get your story straight. When the deadline is less rigid, then you can probably demand more time to thoroughly think the situation through, before talking.

Where Will the Interview be Held?

Does the reporter want to come to your home or where you work? Does the interview only involve you or your whole family? Do you need to check with your spouse, or your employer to make some of the arrangements? You may be willing to talk, but you don't want to do it in front of your boss.

Perhaps you don't want the reporter to show where you live. That could mean doing the interview some place other than at your home, or it could mean asking the reporter to agree not to give your address or show the outside of your house. Shelters for battered women routinely demand that reporters who interview residents not reveal the shelter's location, for obvious reasons.

How Long Will it Take?

An interview can be as brief as 10 or 15 minutes, something you can do at your desk between other appointments. An impromptu interview at the scene of an accident or crime may last just a minute or two. Other stories take much longer. An in-depth piece can take hours, or even days to shoot. Does the reporter want to do an up-close-and-personal piece about you, and shadow you from dusk till dawn? For a week? Ask the reporter for some sort of estimate in advance. Keep in mind that a brief and carefully focused interview can become a rambling "fishing expedition" if it's allowed to continue too long. It's much easier to set a reasonable time limit in advance than it is to try to ask someone to leave once you're on camera.

You may want to arrange for a colleague or assistant to politely intervene and "rescue" you at the appointed hour. That way you don't have to try to cut-off the conversation yourself.

Show and Tell

You no doubt remember this from kindergarten, and the technique hasn't changed much since then. It's now common for television crews to want to show the subjects of stories doing something besides just talking. Instead of interviewing a cop standing beside his car, we may ask to speak with him as we ride along. Rather than have you and your family just line up on a couch, we may want to talk to you while you're watching televised reports on the battle your son is fighting. We may do an interview as you turn on your tap to show us the tainted water that you're upset about. It's a technique that helps make the story more visually interesting. Radio reporters sometimes use a similar technique, to get "natural sound" as well as your voice.

It may seem like a distraction, one more thing you have to think about, but it will usually help you relax. Actors discovered long ago that they look more comfortable if they can find something to do as they talk. It's one reason Hollywood movies once glamorized smoking. A cigarette was a simple prop that could be used in almost any situation to help a character look more natural. Reporters sometimes hold props or make gestures when they do standups for the same reason. It usually works the same way for someone being interviewed.

Such arrangements are usually harmless, but be sure you understand the reporter's expectations. Discussing the benefits of mammography is much easier than demonstrating it.

Is it "Live" or is it...?

In broadcast news the opposite of "live" isn't "dead". (Although when it goes badly, it can make you or I wish we were.) No, it's "taped". There are important differences between interviews that are taped for later broadcast, and interviews that are live as you speak. I'll get into how you should handle both situations in the chapter on interviews. I mention it here only because it's important that you ask in advance which it will be, so you can prepare accordingly.

When There's More Than One Reporter–
Containing the Herd

Reporters have long been criticized for having a "herd mentality", for acting like "a pack of dogs" or "vultures."

They're descriptions that sometimes fit. It can happen in the "heat of battle" for, I think, understandable reasons. But there are other times when we have no one to blame but ourselves.

Near the end of his presidency, Ronald Reagan held a live news conference in the White House press room to announce a tentative arms control agreement with the Soviets. Appearing at the podium, the President offered only a brief announcement, introduced Secretary of State George Schultz, and then turned around and started to leave. Reagan intended to have Schultz do all the talking, but that wasn't what the reporters had in mind. It would be only seconds before the President made a clean getaway. So on live television, they shouted for Reagan's attention.

That much you would have seen at news conferences I've covered with governors. However, this time it went further. Reagan returned to the podium, and looked willing to answer questions, but he couldn't. As I watched my television, first in amazement, then in utter consternation, three White House network correspondents continued shouting. ABC's Sam Donaldson, CBS's Bill Plante and NBC's Chris Wallace were no longer trying to get Reagan's attention. They had that. They were trying to one up each other for that prestigious *first question*, and they kept it up for nearly 20 seconds. The embarrassing din made it impossible for Reagan to respond to any of them. As he stood there, I'm sure he realized who looked foolish, and he began to smile. Schultz laughed. Other reporters just shook their heads. If ever a President had an opportunity to confirm the public's worst suspicions about the media, this was that moment.

As journalists, we all commit our share of sins, both real and perceived. Like the horde of photographers who descended on a clergyman who was merely trying to console a young boy in mourning, during a memorial service for those killed on the U.S.S. Stark. The priest's only mistake–if you choose to call it that–was creating such a compelling image of emotion at a memorial service covered by media from throughout the nation. And throughout the nation is just where that picture went. Did taking it show a lack of sensitivity? Of course it did. But I wouldn't want to be a photographer trying to explain to my boss why I didn't take that picture when I had the chance.

Competition can be a fierce and ruthless motivator. I would argue that those photographers were more justified in their actions than Donaldson, Plante and Wallace. But many would consider the result even more disturbing.

It's easy to criticize *The Media* for such a flagrant intrusion, but please realize that we're not a single organization. We're individuals working for different companies, and part of our job is to try to outdo each other. Print media all over the country ran that picture of the priest consoling that boy. Some of them did a little soul searching first, but knowing that their competitors had it, they decided not to get beat on the story. That's not an excuse for what happened, just an explanation.

Funerals are always tough stories to do. The coverage may look aggressive, but I've met few reporters who enjoy that kind of assignment. By nature, funerals are emotionally charged situations. The people we deal with may be distraught, and such stories are usually competitive, with many news organizations present. If a funeral is of interest to one reporter, it's almost certain to be of interest to everyone.

Many of the problems that come up in these situations can be avoided with a little forethought. When someone expects large numbers of media at a major event, months of planning can go into getting ready for the onslaught.

The professionals who prepare for political conventions and major sporting events go to great lengths to accommodate the press. They're not going to all that trouble and expense simply to be nice to reporters. They do it to control reporters, because they know if they don't, the situation may quickly spin out of anyone's control. Many of the things those professionals do, you may want to do on a smaller scale.

Set Reasonable Restrictions.

Funerals and memorial services are good examples of situations you can control. It's difficult for a reporter to criticize a family that wants its privacy at such a time. So you can generally expect reporters to do what you ask, if you make reasonable attempts to accommodate them. If you decide to allow cameras, you will probably want to restrict them to a specific area inside the service. You may want to "cut a deal" so to speak. For example, you might decide to allow news crews into the main service, with the understanding that they will agree not to cover the graveside ceremonies. That way they get some cooperation in covering the story; and you still get some privacy.

Whatever you decide, *You should make the arrangements clear to each news organization in advance*: "Yes we will allow you into the funeral, only if you will agree to stay away from the cemetery." There are reporters who chafe at such limitations, but few will blatantly break that type of good faith agreement. Most reporters will feel compelled to accept your terms, because to refuse is to risk missing something that the reporter's competitors will have. The key is to make whatever you're willing to do (allow access to the main service) attractive enough to persuade reporters to forgo something else.

Then be cooperative with those who agree, and firm with those who don't.

At any private event, you have the right to simply ban the media, but that can have the undesirable effect of creating a cat-and-mouse game with reporters. You've forfeited the ability to control events, and the result is often unpredictable. A news organization may decide for competitive reasons that it must still do the story. I've had the unpleasant assignment of trying to get pictures of a funeral when I wasn't wanted. That usually means videotaping people entering and leaving, and of the casket and pallbearers, from some vantage point on public property. A story covered that way is likely to be perceived less sensitively than either the family or I would prefer.

The same principles apply to many different situations. If you don't want cameras swarming around your business, consider arranging a specific time to allow them to get the shots they need. If you're being hounded to answer questions, remember that the sooner you try to accommodate those requests, the sooner the demands will end.

News Conferences

Another way to set limits is to call a news conference. It's a way to make reporters work at your convenience. You set the time and place. Keep in mind, however, that you want to maintain the reporter's good will. Your goal should be to accommodate the media, not arbitrarily restrict it. I know this sounds self-serving on my part, but the approach you take when you feel as if you're fending off reporters should be the same approach you would take if you're appealing for their attention. After all, these are the people who will inevitably get the last word. It's a point made by many media targets, from Huey Long to Tommy Lasorda: Don't fight with people who buy ink by the gallon (or videotape by the truckload).

That means you should be sensitive to reporters' deadlines when you schedule a news conference, and sensitive to the logistics involved. If your intent is to gracefully manage the situation, you won't achieve that in a room that is too small or by calling reporters together minutes before they need to be on the air.

Sometimes the most obvious adjustments aren't made, and the result is unnecessary ill will. A few years ago, I was one of dozens of reporters who covered a tragic plane crash in Sioux City, Iowa. United Airlines Flight 232 was disabled and attempted an emergency landing. The pilot had so little control that it was a wonder he ever got to the field. At the last moment the jet caught a wing tip, cartwheeled across the runway and exploded in flames. Miraculously, most of those aboard survived. An exceptionally well-executed emergency response plan saved many lives. The story we told became one of great heroism by many different individuals, and by the community as a whole. Unfortunately, the media was not always managed so well.

Within hours of the crash of Flight 232, news crews and satellite trucks converged on Sioux City from all over the country. At one news conference I counted more than 30 television cameras, plus still-photographers and scores of reporters. The city manager was our main source of information about the crash during the first 48 hours or so. He held several impromptu news conferences in the airport terminal, and with so many crews all trying to get pictures at once, it didn't always go smoothly. Anyone walking in unannounced to talk to reporters, risked being smothered by cameras and microphones jockeying for position. It had the potential to be "pack journalism" at its worst. None of us like working that way, but no one wants to have to explain to the boss why the competition got videotape but, "I couldn't."

The morning following the crash a news conference was scheduled "at the terminal," but no specific arrangements were made. It was simply left to the press corps to be ready. We're accustomed to making the best of less-than-ideal circumstances, so we made some collective decisions intended to make all our jobs a little easier. We chose a spot with plenty of room, and created a huge arc of cameras. We thought we were being helpful, but we might as well have saved ourselves the trouble.

When the city manager appeared, he walked up to the podium flanked by two uniformed law-enforcement officers. These "bodyguards" were apparently intended to prevent any overly aggressive reporters from getting too close, and they were right out of central casting. They didn't speak. They didn't look anyone in the eye. They just marched in and stood to either side *in front* of the person we wanted to see. Each of them blocked or partially blocked the view of several cameras, one of which was mine. They stayed there through the whole news conference, despite constant appeals for them to move. Those reporters who were able to get their shots, asked questions, fearing they too might soon lose the opportunity. Those of us who couldn't, pleaded with the "hired guns" to move and wondered out loud about the sheer idiocy of calling a news conference and then preventing reporters from covering it. The city manager simply ignored our protests. He proceeded as though there was no problem, and offered no explanation.

To this day, I've never found any logic in how he handled the situation. I've wondered if he was genuinely afraid of us, or felt that dealing with us was just some unimportant chore. Maybe he shared the perception held by so many people that we were some unruly horde to be dealt with, but never appeased. He couldn't have been thinking about all the people nationwide who were learning what had happened through our efforts.

The purpose of a news conference should be to facilitate the flow of information between you and the public. Don't let your perceptions about reporters cause you to lose sight of that overriding goal.

There's no great mystery about setting up a news conference. Make sure the room is big enough, there's enough power for a few of our lights, a place to put microphones, and you usually have it covered. If you expect a large number of cameras, you may need some risers. Make sure you have a pleasant looking background and you're all set. You can get fancy, with your logo on the podium. A sound distribution system is helpful, but unless you're expecting a crowd, it's not essential. We really don't expect much, just the ability to clearly see and hear whoever is talking.

"Next!"

Another approach that works in some situations is to schedule a series of one-on-one interviews. I've seen it used effectively by public officials and occasionally by private executives. Sometimes newsmakers will inadvertently do a series of interviews because they started saying, "Yes," before they knew how many reporters would call.

It's a technique that offers some unique advantages. You may feel more comfortable dealing with individuals than with a room full of cameras and people asking questions. If the topic of the story is sensitive, this is a good way to use some friendly persuasion. If the subject is complex, you can craft your remarks to fit each reporter's level of expertise. Some may need more "educating" than others. Maybe you suspect that some reporters will be friendlier than others and you don't want one reporter's aggression at a news conference to make others any less sympathetic.

You also minimize any "cross fertilization" between reporters. Not every reporter may know every relevant fact about the story. Maybe no one reporter has the whole picture, and you'd prefer to keep it that way. If you hold a news conference, reporters sometimes learn a lot from each other's questions. Doing each interview separately prevents that. It's an advantage you lose once everyone sees each other's stories. Still, by that time some of those stories may have a more favorable "angle" or "spin" than they would if all the reporters heard each other beforehand.

Another benefit is that if you make an ill-advised statement, not everyone hears it. At worst only one reporter will have that quotation. If you're inexperienced or unsure of what to expect, a series of interviews can be a great way to learn from your mistakes. What happens in one interview can help you better prepare for the next one.

Reporters frequently prefer to do one-on-one interviews. If I have facts I don't want to share, it's difficult to get a source to respond to them at a news conference without tipping off my competitors. I mentioned earlier that television crews often like to have people doing something as they're being interviewed. A news conference makes that impossible. Given a choice, I'd much prefer to talk to a newsworthy hospital patient in his or her room and get some pictures of that person being treated. Likewise, sitting down with the Governor or a company president in a couple of leather armchairs adds a certain cachet to my story that I can't get at a news conference. Even when I know other reporters have had the same conversation, I can still add a hint of exclusivity to my story. I can say, "*I* spoke with...," rather than, "We..."

The biggest drawback to this approach is that it can take a considerable amount of your time. It works best when you're dealing with several reporters, but not a crowd. In many cities, you can meet with three or four television reporters, one or two newspaper folks, a couple from radio, and have it covered. If the list is much longer than that, it may not be workable. Sometimes only a few reporters will call on a story and it makes sense to set several appointments.

I have seen situations where a governor will conduct a series of television interviews, or a company will call together only print reporters. Such arrangements are rare and they usually draw complaints from whoever's not included. The resulting ill will may outweigh any benefits you hope to gain by focusing on only one group.

All Right, Everyone Into the "Pool".

Occasionally I've asked someone for an interview or perhaps for a snapshot of some family member, and they say, "Can't you get what I said from the reporter for channel __? I already did that for them." The answer is usually, "No, I can't." Competing reporters don't share. However, we do sometimes "pool". The difference is whether we've made any arrangements *in advance*. We almost never exchange recorded material unless we've agreed to do so beforehand.

Pool agreements are usually made at the request of the source. It may be totally impractical to allow every reporter and camera into someone's hospital room. Instead, the patient will sometimes agree to let in one camera. The understanding is that the reporter will give copies of whatever is videotaped to everyone else. When Soviet President Gorbachev visited Minnesota, the Governor's staff worked with the television stations in town to create an elaborate system of pools. Each station agreed to shoot at one or more key locations and then feed the pictures to everyone. The major networks take turns being the "pool camera" for Presidential addresses.

There are other less formal arrangements. When we ask relatives for a picture of perhaps a child killed in a fire, the family may want to be sure that it will be "shared". That way they don't have to handle so many separate requests. To do that, you simply insist *before you give out the picture* that the first reporter who asks for it make it available to others. Some people keep the picture in their possession and let everyone photograph or videotape it in their home.

A pool is one way for you to avoid doing a news conference, and still have to do just one interview. You may want to choose one reporter you're comfortable with, or let the interested reporters decide among themselves. The important thing is to arrange a pool before the interview or event. When a reporter already has material on tape, that reporter has no obligation to you or to the other reporters to share it, if there was no agreement made to do so. After all, we're competitors. Part of our job is to be the first to get the story.

You may want to clarify whether the pool arrangement is to be "total" or "partial". A reporter will sometimes try to gain an advantage over competitors by first doing a pool interview, then record additional questions on a separate tape—for his or her exclusive use. Allowing that is a way for you to favor a reporter whom you like, or who called first. But it's a tactic sure to draw charges of unfairness from other reporters. If you want to avoid that problem, it's a good idea to make it clear that everything you say is to be part of the pool.

* * *

All of this is not intended to suggest that it's your responsibility to play referee for a bunch of journalists. What you decide to do should be whatever makes the situation easiest for you to handle, not what some reporter demands. These are some of the ways to do that and still keep everyone reasonably happy. That should in turn give you fewer hassles before the story airs and hopefully a more favorable result when it does.

An important thing to remember whenever you set limits is to be consistent. Whatever boundaries you set for one reporter, place on all reporters. (I'm starting to sound as if I'm giving advice for handling small children—which may be a good analogy.) We're more likely to accept your limitations if you assure us that you won't let a competitor beat us. Also be sure you're not sending mixed signals. If you're setting restrictions at a funeral, be sure everyone in the family understands and agrees. If you arrange to allow access to your company, be sure you notify all employees. You can quickly lose a reporter's good will by agreeing to do something and then having someone else contradict you.

CHAPTER FIVE:

WHEN YOU DON'T WANT TO TALK

You have every right not to talk to a reporter. But a decision not to talk can be risky, sometimes more risky than talking. You want to be sure you've thought through the situation carefully.

Several years ago when I was Business Editor, I did a story about Northwest Airlines. At that time Northwest had a reputation among Minneapolis/St. Paul reporters as the single most difficult company with which we had to work. (It has since changed ownership and management, and–like Control Data–dramatically improved its media relations.) The company was notorious for restricting access to reporters, refusing to provide information, and sometimes failing to even return phone calls. All that from what was a publicly held company that is one of the state's largest employers and which is frequently in the news.

I'd had run-ins with Northwest before, but this time the airline reached a new level of inept media management. The story was about a Supreme Court ruling in a sex discrimination lawsuit against Northwest. Years before, female flight attendants for the airline had filed the suit alleging that Northwest paid some male crew members more than women, for doing what was really the same job. It had been in the courts for years. My story was that the company had finally lost the lawsuit on appeal. That meant hundreds of female flight attendants would finally get their money. The settlements for back pay totaled as much as tens of thousands of dollars in some cases.

Northwest had long since discontinued the discriminatory practices, and had admitted they were wrong. Its defense in court was that the discrimination wasn't intentional. The airline argued that since it had been corrected, the court shouldn't penalize the airline.

As I mentally figured how I would put the story together, I imagined using a quotation from someone with the company explaining what its defense had been. The airline could legitimately say it had already made corrections and perhaps say it regretted the whole affair. I would also, of course, interview some flight attendants about how happy they must be to get such a windfall.

I started by calling Northwest. I explained the story I was doing and asked for an interview. I also asked to speak with some flight attendants. To both requests I got a flat refusal. The airline would do nothing. It wasn't even releasing a statement. Okay, that meant I would say something like, "Northwest Airlines has no comment on the ruling." But I still needed flight attendants. That meant going to the airport.

Northwest controls entire concourses leading to its gates. The company had a standing policy not to allow any television cameras into those areas without advance permission–which I didn't have. There are, however, public areas just outside each concourse through which flight crews must pass. So a photographer and I positioned ourselves at one of those entrances looking for flight attendants. Sure enough, some soon headed our way and I asked them to do an interview. They declined, so I asked others and eventually found someone willing to talk, but not before a man interrupted us. He didn't identity himself; he just insisted that we couldn't be there.

At first I didn't know who he was. As we spoke off-camera, I explained that we were in a public area, and he had no authority to stop us. From what he said, I suspected I was dealing with more than just an amateur security guard; he apparently knew why we were there before he approached us. After we talked awhile, he finally admitted he was a manager for Northwest.

After our less-than-friendly exchange he left. But within minutes he returned, with several other Northwest people. They fanned out to cover every access point to where we were standing. Then they stopped any Northwest employees as they approached and told them not to talk to us. Seeing what they were doing, I turned to the photographer and said, "Okay, let's roll."

With the camera on this time, we approached the man just as he was speaking to a flight crew. Pushing the microphone toward him, I asked, "What's the problem here?" He turned to me, obviously enraged, and blurted out,

YOU'RE DAMN-WELL NOT GOING TO TALK TO ANYONE FROM NORTHWEST!!!

In that brief moment, he took an average ho-hum story that we might have buried somewhere in the middle of a newscast, and turned it into the hottest story of the day. (It also raised my stock a little with my bosses.) That sentence ran in every show we had on the air that night, with a strategically located "BEEP!" in the middle of it. It was every show producer's favorite on-air tease, so it often ran more than once during a newscast. We also used it for promotional spots during prime time programming. In short, it was a public relations disaster for Northwest Airlines.

Now before you call those producers and me cynical and insensitive, please realize that the remark simply put into words what I already knew was the company's attitude toward my requests for information and assistance. That he delivered it with so much enthusiasm, and on camera, made it irresistibly good television. Television works best when it personalizes ideas that are otherwise abstract. I couldn't have done that better if I'd scripted his remarks myself.

How could it have been prevented? Not with a policy banning employees from speaking to reporters. It was just such a policy that one inept employee was trying to enforce. The obvious solution would have been to cooperate in the first place. The company could easily have provided someone to do a brief interview. Someone accustomed to dealing with a reporter could have articulated the company's position. It was a position I considered reasonable under the circumstances (much more reasonable than the refusal to talk about it). Yes, we still would have interviewed some flight attendants, but what could any one of them have said that would have been remotely as damaging as the attempt to stop us? The most harmful information we had was that the company lost the lawsuit. That much we would have reported if the story was only one sentence long, until Northwest gave us a better sentence.

WHAT'S YOUR RATIONALE?

You want to think carefully about why you don't want to talk. Can you explain to yourself why that's a wise course of action? Can you explain it to the reporter?

"I Want My Privacy."

The topic may be so personal or disturbing to you that you simply don't feel comfortable discussing it in public. If that's true, say so. It's hard for any reporter to argue with someone who's lost a loved one and doesn't want to talk about it. We may try to gently persuade you to talk, but no one's likely to get antagonistic. There's no reason for the story to treat you unfavorably because you didn't cooperate. On the other hand, do you want the public to have a favorable impression of the person you've lost? Can you give them that by talking?

"It's Confidential."

Even the most aggressive reporter recognizes that some information simply isn't public. The issue usually comes down to exactly where you draw the line. Perhaps your company is about to undergo a merger and is in the midst of sensitive negotiations. A reporter calls and says there's a rumor going around about a possible takeover. It's certainly a good story to the reporter. There's legitimate public interest. It may affect thousands of employees and investors. But if you say anything now, it could jeopardize the whole transaction. If you lie, you may be caught in it—or worse; a false statement about a securities transaction can be a criminal offense! Not talking may seem like the smartest approach. But what if the reporter already has enough information to go ahead with the story? Do you want to have some influence? Are there errors that could be damaging if they're not corrected? A discreet conversation, with perhaps part of it "for background only," might be a lesser evil than refusing to talk at all.

"I Don't Have Time."

Reporters usually need something, "Yesterday." Most of the stories any of us do, we do on a daily routine. By tomorrow it's not "news" anymore. That means we're almost certain to ask you to change your schedule. You have to decide whether it's worth the imposition. Is the story so valuable or so potentially damaging that your response is necessary? If you're busy, is there someone else on your staff who can do it?

Lack of time may seem like a convenient "out". It's tempting to say, "I can't talk, I'm in meetings all day." (Or have your administrative assistant say it for you.) But all that matters to the reporter is that you've refused to talk, and that's generally what we'll say in the story. Any attempts to stall probably won't delay the story, and may result in one that's less favorable. You need to ask yourself whether the time and effort required to help the reporter make deadline, is less than the time required to control the damage later.

"My Attorney Says..."

Sometimes people facing criminal charges or lawsuits are advised by their attorney not to talk to the media. So when a reporter calls the response is, "My attorney says I shouldn't comment." Often it doesn't even get that far; someone's secretary or spouse will take the call and refuse to put it through. They'll give me the name of some attorney who's, "Handling all questions from reporters." I've had sources ask me to call their attorney, to explain exactly what I want, before they agree to talk. Sometimes the attorney agrees to talk instead.

My experience is that attorneys tend to be very conservative about what to say to a reporter. Your lawyer's worst nightmare is that some clever reporter will get you to publicly incriminate yourself by admitting to some fact that is damaging to your case.

That's understandable, but most attorneys have very little experience dealing directly with the media, and may not be considering all the implications. Does your attorney understand that perhaps you're losing professional clients every day that goes by without an adequate public response from you? Are you starting to look like a pariah in your community, without any way to counter those impressions?

A few lawyers are skilled at handling the media, and recognize that a reporter can be an ally at times. For example, if you're suing a major company for negligence, the company knows it may take you years to get to court. It also knows that it only takes hours to get the story on television or in the newspaper. Publicity may be far more damaging to the company than any potential settlement with you, so it's a way for you to apply pressure. Some lawsuits are settled quickly out of court to avoid adverse publicity.

At other times, your attorney's motives may be more self-serving. Publicity about one lawsuit will often bring others to the same attorney or law firm. Once, after an airline disaster, I interviewed a lawyer with a firm that was filing the first lawsuit on behalf of a victim of the crash. I arrived a little early, and was offered some coffee. As I sipped from a china cup surrounded by elegantly paneled walls on the top floor of the tallest building in the state, I asked a member of the firm why he had contacted us. He casually explained to me (off camera) that this was a, "race for publicity." The first firm to get its name on television, he explained, has the best chance of attracting more lawsuits from other crash victims. (I was amazed only by his candor.) Under such circumstances, you may not want to be in the spotlight. You may want to keep your privacy, despite what, "My attorney says..."

Some attorneys are "legalbrilliant" but "mediadumb". If you have reason to expect media attention involving legal matters, you should have a detailed discussion with your lawyer about just what is in your best interests. You may want to seek professional media advice from someone with that expertise, and let your attorney stick to his specialty–defending you in court.

EXPLAIN YOURSELF.

No, you don't have to justify your actions to any and every reporter who wants to know, but you probably should whenever possible. Remember, this is someone who will do a story that is either going to be favorable or unfavorable to you. It's also someone who will become more suspicious the more reluctant you are to cooperate. Even just a brief explanation of why you can't answer questions, is usually better than, "No comment." You're giving yourself a chance to influence the story, and you just may be able to win the reporter's sympathy.

If your attorney doesn't want you to talk, say so. Make him or her the heavy. If there are sensitive negotiations underway with companies you can't name, perhaps you can say just that and use that as the reason to say nothing more. If you're ever unfortunate enough to have a loved one die in a way that makes news, you'll get calls from reporters. (We don't like making them anymore than you like getting them, but we will.) You can simply say this is a time when your family wants privacy. You may continue to get media requests, but only a fool would publicly berate you for turning them down.

If there is no reason you can give the reporter, at least be sure there's one you can give yourself. If your only justification is, "It might make me look bad," think again. The reporter may do that anyway, with or without your help. The question you should ask yourself is, "Is there anything I can do to avoid looking bad?"

DON'T LIE.

There is one situation when not talking is always preferable. If you honestly feel that anything you can say will be a lie, then don't speak (Great Rule #2). If you really did abuse some poor child or rob a bank, then you may have little to gain by talking about it. Saying something that will later demonstrate that you're a liar too won't help much. (Remember what happened to Control Data.) For politicians or others in a position of public trust, making up excuses can be more damaging than the original offense. As your mother used to say, "Lying about it will only make it worse."

BEWARE OF THE BLUFF.

There's a bit of reporter sophistry that works occasionally on some unsuspecting source. It goes something like this: The reporter hears a rumor, or maybe just someone's speculation that something has happened or soon will. The problem is that the reporter isn't sure whether it's true or not. The only way to find out is to ask the person involved–you. Since the story isn't very flattering, you aren't likely to confirm anything if you can avoid it. What does the reporter do? The reporter calls you and pretends to already know.

Instead of saying, "Are you being accused of sexual harassment?," the reporter says something like, "I understand you're being charged with sexual harassment," or, "I'd like to get your response to the accusations of sexual harassment that have been made against you." The idea is to give you the impression that the reporter already knows it's true, so you'll confirm it. We know that you may flatly deny that it's true or claim that you know nothing about it. (In a reporter's mind, those answers will mean that it's still unconfirmed.) We also know that you just might respond, and we will have accomplished two things: confirmed the rumor, and obtained your reaction.

If it's any consolation, many reporters condemn this kind of deception. But that doesn't stop others from practicing it.

If you try to call the bluff by asking where the reporter got the information, the answer you'll get depends on the ethics of the reporter and the importance of the story. Some reporters will avoid an outright lie and confess that it's just a rumor. Others will try to maintain the ruse, saying perhaps that they can't name a "confidential source".

What should you do? First, always ask who the reporter's other sources are, and exactly what information he or she already knows. (See chapter 3.) Even a partial answer to those questions could be enlightening. Second, try not to give the reporter any new facts, even by implication. Third, don't confirm rumors or speculation.

The nagging problem for you is: How do you know for sure if it's really a bluff? The answer is: You don't. The reporter may really have a confidential source. Even if there isn't such a source, if the rumor's true how long will it be before this reporter or another one confirms it some other way? You may want to go ahead and give your side of the story.

The bluff doesn't have to be about the whole story. The reporter may use it to try to get you to confirm some uncertain fact. It may be an attempt to provoke you: "So-and-so said you did this..." The reporter may hope you'll admit to certain charges if you think that they've already been corroborated. Be careful not to let yourself jump to conclusions based solely on what the reporter asserts to be true. We don't take your word at face value, and you shouldn't always take our word as the truth either. It may not be.

Unfortunately for you, the reporter can take liberties you can't. A dishonest reporter's deceptions are not likely to ever be public. Your deceptions could be in the headlines. (Life isn't fair.) The safest course is always to state the truth as you know it. That includes being willing to say, "I don't know," if that's the truth. Again, if you're tempted to lie about the situation, think carefully, and ask yourself how you'll look once everyone knows the truth.

BEWARE THE "BAIT AND SWITCH."

Another ploy some reporters use, is to tell you they're doing a story about one thing, and then hit you with unexpected questions about something entirely different. It's a favorite tactic of investigative reporters. The commander of U.S. forces in Vietnam, General William Westmoreland, filed a famous lawsuit against CBS, accusing Correspondent Mike Wallace and his producer of using just such a tactic in an interview with the general. It was just one of many charges and counter charges in Westmoreland's $120-million libel suit against CBS. The interview was part of a documentary, called *The Uncounted Enemy: A Vietnam Deception*. The story's central premise was that Westmoreland and other U.S. commanders in Vietnam conspired to undercount the number of enemy soldiers. They allegedly did it to minimize the perceived threat, and maintain public support for the war effort.

Westmoreland contended that questions about the enemy troop estimates were sprung on him during an interview that he had been told would be a retrospective of his years in Southeast Asia–a personal profile. Furthermore, Westmoreland said his attempts to respond were taken out of context, making him look like he was lying, rather than simply unprepared. CBS stood by the story, and the case went to trial. The courtroom drama lasted 18 weeks, but Westmoreland and CBS reached a settlement just before jury deliberations.

I've known reporters who've targeted someone for a story and made up complete fabrications to get pictures and an interview. In one such case, a reporter told a farmer he'd won an award for his veal calf operation, when the intended story was an exposé on animal abuse.

Sometimes the reporter is just very vague about the thrust of the story. A doctor might be told that the story is about his particular specialty and he's needed as an "illustration", when the intended story is about malpractice.

This is another practice many reporters condemn. Such tactics don't do much to build trust in the media. While you're cursing us under your breath, here are a few suggestions for how to deal with such ploys.

Surprise!

Reporters tend to hold to the ethic that any question is fair, at any time. During his many years covering the White House, Sam Donaldson made it a practice to ask questions whenever the President was within earshot. It didn't matter that the occasion was supposed to be just a "photo opportunity" or that he had to yell over the roar of a helicopter; he asked. And he often got an answer. Those of us who cover state capitals sometimes attend the most routine announcements by governors–things we know we'll never use–because it's a chance to ask questions about something else. Governors and presidents understand this. That's why they often come to minor events prepared to answer questions about some pressing story. That's also why they can be so hard to find when they're's involved in some controversy.

There is no foolproof way to defend against such media tactics. The best advice I can give you is ask plenty of questions beforehand, and try to deal with reporters you trust. If you know of some topic that might give the reporter an ulterior motive, and you still think you should do the interview, *be prepared to discuss that topic.* Be sure you can answer any questions that are relevant to the subject of the interview, or be able to give a good reason why you can't. In other words, ***Do your homework.***

Cool, Calm and Collected

If a reporter does a "switch" on you during an interview, above all *maintain your composure.* Nothing will shake your credibility faster than losing your temper, stammering or storming out of the room. That's exactly what the reporter wants you to do. A dramatic response only enhances the story.

Like an attorney cross-examining a witness, the reporter is probing for any sign of weakness, any body language that betrays a lie. If you give us that moment of consternation, that is exactly what will appear in the story. Count on it. The reporter may be a total jerk, but responding in kind is the worst thing you can do. By the time a taped interview becomes part of a story, what the reporter did or said is long since on the editing room floor. You're the one who looks flustered. Some reporters will deliberately try to provoke you into an emotional outburst. When you lose your composure, you're giving them exactly what they want.

The same rules apply in a live situation, when viewers can see how you're being treated. If the interviewer wants to look like a jerk, let him. When you lower yourself to the same level, you forfeit any viewer sympathy that you might otherwise have gained.

It's equally true in print or radio, where there's usually no clue to how the reporter may have approached you; only how you reacted.

You don't have to be an easy mark. If you don't know something, say so. If possible, explain why you don't know. If it's information you can find, offer to get back to the reporter with it. If you have no other alternative, politely explain that you did not know that the new topic was to be the subject of the interview and say you're not prepared to comment. Restate your position *once* if the reporter presses you, but don't repeat the same sentence over and over; you'll soon sound like you're, "taking the Fifth".

Setting Limits in Advance.

It's sometimes possible to demand that the reporter not ask about a certain sensitive subject, before the interview starts. It's an arrangement that's used when both the source and the reporter know what that other subject is, but the reporter is doing some other story or doesn't need those comments. Judges rarely do interviews on cases that they're hearing, but I've known judges who will explain the complexities of the judicial process as it affects some case. They might explain what some ruling means in terms that a layperson can understand. It's done with the clear understanding that the judge can't comment on any of the issues of the case.

Reporters rarely object to that kind of legitimate restriction. Anything as strong as the requirements of judicial canons should convince even the most suspicious reporter. If you can make a case that certain questions are too sensitive and are not crucial to the story, we may agree. If we don't, you can still refuse to do the interview.

Some media consultants advise that you always limit the scope of any interview to not more than a few topics. With an advance agreement, you at least have something to point to when you decline to answer. As I mentioned above, you can say something like, "I didn't come prepared to discuss that matter, because I didn't think it would be a part of this interview." However, that won't carry much weight if it's a factual question about your own actions, or anything that you would obviously know anyway.

Keep in mind that talking about some previous "deal" on camera may not leave the best impression either. When you clearly have the information, and don't intend to disclose it, the only safe course is to be prepared to state your reasons for withholding it, during the interview. Often a reporter who's acting in good faith will ask you to state your reasons on camera, just to make sure that your rationale is "on the record".

JUST GIVE US A "TASTE".

One way to keep reporters at bay is to throw us a few scraps. Sometimes giving us just enough to let us do our stories will satisfy our cravings. If you can find something to offer, perhaps just a few brief remarks, that will often stop the calls and questions at least for a while.

Months after Minnesota's most famous child-abduction had faded from the daily headlines, someone discovered a body floating in the Mississippi River. Investigators had few remaining leads in the Jacob Wetterling case. The body was found in Minneapolis downstream from where an abductor could conceivably have put Jacob, and it was the body of a boy about Jacob's age. We first heard about it hours before authorities could make a positive identification, but both investigators and reporters assumed it must be him.

While other reporters followed the recovery of the body, I went to see Jacob's family in nearby St. Joseph. I'd become closer to the Wetterlings than anyone else on our staff, so I had the dubious assignment of finding out if they would talk. I wanted something on videotape if possible, so I didn't try to call first. When I got to the house, I told the photographer to wait in the car. If I was going to get an interview, it wouldn't be by being pushy. I knocked on the door and a friend of the Wetterlings answered. The house was packed with friends and family. Several people I knew greeted me, but they didn't invite me in. Then I saw Jacob's mother at the top of the stairs. In the most sympathetic voice I could muster, I said something like:

"Hello Patty. You know why I'm here. We all hope it's not him. Do you feel like talking about it?"

Without coming down the stairs, and with complete composure, she said:

"It's not Jacob. I know it's not him, and I won't believe it's him until somebody proves it to me."

When I did a live report from outside the Wetterling home on the news that night, I didn't have any interview or new pictures to show, but I had a quotation. I said I'd spoken with the family and I repeated Patty Wetterling's words. It was just enough. I later discovered she had made the same remarks to every reporter who called or stopped by that night. She had been careful to be consistent so no reporter felt slighted, and she had given all of us something we could use. She managed to maintain her family's privacy at an extremely trying time, yet still kept the media's good will.

She was also correct about Jacob. We later learned that the body wasn't his.

Many situations lend themselves to this approach. Grieving families sometimes ask a close friend or member of the clergy to speak on their behalf. Companies may issue brief written statements. Police and fire investigators will frequently do short interviews at the scene of a crime or accident.

It can also be a way to respond to allegations without being drawn into a lengthy debate. During labor disputes, it's usually the union that has the most to say to reporters. Most companies seem to have concluded long ago that rhetoric about things like fair wages and better working conditions plays to public sympathies better than a business's need to maintain profits. So while employees picket, most employers prefer to negotiate behind closed doors. The difficulty for reporters covering strikes is that we need to get both sides.

When the reporting staff of the *Star Tribune* called a strike several years ago, management held several news conferences. I'm sure the company realized how hypocritical it would look for a media company to shun the reporters who were covering the walkout. We never got much information from them. Executives would say that they were always ready and willing to negotiate and then they might vaguely outline some issues, but they offered little else. They were always careful to say, "We don't want to negotiate this dispute in public," and declined to answer any questions that might lead them to do that. In reality they were saying almost nothing newsworthy, but no one's story ever said, "The newspaper refuses to talk."

Sometimes you don't have to give very much, to maintain good relations with reporters, if you can justify where you want to draw the line.

HYPOTHETICALLY SPEAKING

There are times when sources genuinely want to provide information, but can't for legal reasons (Great Rule #3). It may be a police investigator talking about a juvenile offender, a prosecutor discussing secret grand jury proceedings, or an employer being questioned about a fired worker. Reporters recognize that sometimes you can't disclose certain information, but we still need to accurately cover what's happened.

One way you can help us is by agreeing to speak "hypothetically". In other words, don't tell us about the case in question. Just explain how cases like it are normally handled. We will appreciate your assistance, and you may assure that the story won't be wrong or misleading.

A word of caution: I'm not saying you should respond to a reporter's questions about something that hasn't happened. Questions that begin, "What would you do if..." sometimes paint scenarios that may never occur. The handlers of public officials routinely tell them not to answer such "hypotheticals". For a time, one of the favorite ploys of reporters at live presidential news conferences was to concoct false policy dilemmas. The details vary, but the questions generally fit the form of an old parlor game, which asked things like:

"If your spouse and your child are both drowning, and you only have one life preserver, who would you save?"

Those kinds of hypothetical questions, no one should have to answer.

PRIVATE PROPERTY/PUBLIC ACCESS

If you intend to avoid reporters, or restrict where their cameras can go, you need to know where we legally can and cannot be. Despite the impression some people apparently have of reporters charging into unsuspecting people's living rooms, we do not have a right to do that. It's called trespassing. It was illegal long before cameras were invented. It's still illegal. Hopefully it always will be. You decide who's allowed into your home. Any business or property owner has the right to control who enters that property.

At the other end of the spectrum are public streets, where you have almost no right to interfere with a reporter. You can't stop us from taking a picture of your house or your children—unless there's a telephoto lens peering into your bedroom. As a rule, we can photograph or videotape anything that someone can see with the naked eye from public property.

Between those two extremes is considerable gray area. We can't just enter you house, but it's less clear whether a reporter or camera appearing in your yard is an intrusion—until you say so. Anywhere the general public can be is a place that we can sometimes capture on film or video, even if it's technically private property. Quasi-public areas such as airports, shopping malls, hotels, hospitals, government buildings, even your reception room or office are all potential targets for the media. Those same sorts of public accommodations are places where property owners sometimes attempt to restrict media access.

If you don't want cameras in an area where the public is otherwise welcome, you need to make that clear. You need to be vigilant about it. If we suspect that you may deny us access to some otherwise public location, the reporter or photographer will sometimes just walk in. Then we get whatever we can before someone orders us out. We know that once you tell us to leave private property, we have to go, so we delay asking.

If a reporter ignores your firm and unequivocal order to leave your property, you may have grounds for a lawsuit. A sign stating clearly that no cameras are allowed has the same effect, as long as you always enforce it against everybody. A sign has the added benefit of prohibiting hidden cameras, which you might not otherwise detect. Cameras are now so compact that they're easy to conceal, but that doesn't mean they're not subject to the same legal restrictions. Some states have laws specifically governing the use of hidden cameras but most permit them. Most states also apply a standard of "reasonable expectation of privacy", which means that hidden cameras are legally taboo in places like a public rest room, or your hospital room without your permission.

All of this is useful information if you want to conceal your property, but what if it's *you* we want? You can prevent cameras from entering your home or office, but how long can you stay there? How long before you'll have to enter some public place, perhaps to go to your car? If a determined reporter wants to get your picture, or do an ambush interview, there's usually a way to do it without ever entering anyone's private property. (Just ask Madonna or Cher.) Thankfully, most of us will never have to worry about the paparazzi, but any time you're in a public place, we're generally free to take your picture.

If it's you the cameras are after, it may be easier to simply cooperate. You'll probably come across better if you're not being chased down the street. If you're in a public place and you're not the target of the story, then just politely ask us not to "shoot" you, and in most cases we won't. Many times all we're doing is taking pictures of shoppers in a mall, or students on campus, and there are plenty of other people we can use.

* * *

If this chapter sounds as if I'm still trying to persuade you to cooperate, I am. I honestly believe that when you look at most situations carefully, there are very few good reasons not to talk to a reporter. It's risky, but it's usually less risky than the alternatives.

There's one reason for talking I haven't mentioned. It's one reporters rarely use because it sounds so threatening. But a friend of mine, who advises major companies on media relations, says he finds that it's often his most persuasive argument:

If you're not willing to talk, you have very little right to complain later.

You're giving us a tremendous license, because no matter what issues you may raise after the story appears, the reporter can always say, "Hey, I tried to talk to you." Keep in mind that talking doesn't mean you have to say everything you know. There's plenty of room between "stonewalling" and "spilling your guts". You may have good reasons for not answering particular questions, but you can still answer others or talk in generalities. Anytime you're willing to engage a reporter in any small way, you gain potential influence. When you refuse, you forfeit any chance to do that.

CHAPTER SIX:

GETTING YOUR STORY TOLD

Knowing how to respond to a reporter isn't always enough. You may need to somehow attract our interest. Perhaps you know of a problem that isn't being addressed, or you want to make your opinions heard on some pressing issue. You or your organization may be holding an event you want covered. For whatever reasons, you've decided that you want to "go public". If you wait around passively for some reporter to discover your story, you may wait a long time.

How do you persuade a reporter to do your story? You have to find a way to sell it the same way a good salesperson sells anything. You figure out what the reporter needs and then find a way to meet that need. Let me get radical for a moment and suggest that you think of

the reporter as your client or customer. The analogy may
sound presumptuous coming from a reporter, but in many
respects it isn't so far fetched. Approaching a reporter
about doing a story is a lot like trying to become
someone's supplier. There are plenty of stories we can
cover besides yours, just as any business can obtain office
supplies or accounting services somewhere else. What's so
great about your product?

In this chapter, I venture more into the realm of
traditional public relations, but in a more cooperative way
than it's sometimes practiced. I want to help you find
those areas where your interests and the reporter's
interests converge, so you can use them to make yourself
heard.

Reporters brag about stories we've covered. Public
relations professionals brag about "events" they've staged,
or stories they successfully "sold". When professionals are
looking for a reporter to do a story, they call it "shopping
the story around." (The grammar is twisted, but the
analogy holds.) When they succeed, they tend to sound
like the fisher who landed a big one. Their account of the
feat often includes what "bait" they used to get us to
"bite".

GORBY MANIA

One of the cleverest and yet simplest techniques I've
seen used to get on the news was devised by a former U.S.
senator and his staff. (You might have guessed it would be
a politician.) All it took was a little careful timing. The
ploy was so successful that it briefly upstaged a governor
during one of his most glorious moments, as he was
hosting the head of the Soviet Union.

In June 1990, Soviet President Mikhail Gorbachev visited the Twin Cities. It was his first visit to any city in the U.S. outside Washington, which made it very big news in Minnesota. It was also a major political triumph for then Minnesota Governor Rudy Perpich. Perpich had been the butt of more than a few snickers when he dared invite the Soviet Premier to visit. When Gorbachev accepted the invitation, the snickering stopped. It set the stage for an election-year performance that was sure to boost the Governor's standing in the polls. The visit would be a huge media event and the Governor's staff set out to take the best possible political advantage of it.

That meant a carefully crafted guest list of the Governor's supporters, contributors and fellow Democrats. It also meant the careful exclusion of any Republicans–notably U.S. Senator Rudy Boschwitz, who was also up for re-election. The strategy was to make sure that visually and otherwise, the Governor appeared as close to Gorbachev as possible, and any political adversaries be kept as far away as possible.

The atmosphere leading up to the event was politically charged for weeks. At one point it was rumored that Boschwitz tried to persuade President Bush to somehow cancel any Gorbachev stop in Minnesota. Boschwitz feared it was helping Perpich too much.

Local television stations decided to provide live continuous coverage of the visit, which was to last several hours. We knew that events such as Gorbachev's arrival at the airport and his motorcade would be relatively easy to follow. We also knew that during much of the visit, Gorbachev and the Governor would be in meetings, behind closed doors. So we would have to find creative ways to fill the time when cameras couldn't see what's happening. We would need background pieces and interviews with experts, perhaps hours worth. No one knew in advance exactly when it would be necessary to fill time or for how long. We would have to improvise as we went along.

Boschwitz's staff knew there was one time when we would surely need to fill. It would be during a formal dinner held in Gorbachev's honor at the Governor's mansion. Every station had a reporter and camera position outside, but they weren't allowed in–and neither was Boschwitz. The Governor wasn't about to share the spotlight with any rivals so the guest list for the main table didn't include the Senator. Republicans and others with less favor with the Governor were invited, but they were seated in a separate room.

Senator Boschwitz was determined not to be ignored, so he and his staff devised a strategy to steal some of the attention. It worked like this: Once all the dignitaries were inside, Boschwitz headed outside and proceeded to "just stop by" each of the reporters stationed there. Would they like to talk to him? Of course! It was a perfect way for stations to fill time, and discuss a little of the political intrigue surrounding the whole event.

The Senator's press secretary had even arranged to have another staff member watching the various local TV stations at a remote location. Using a two-way radio they then guided the Senator to a reporter with whichever station appeared to have the most time to fill at the moment. The result was lengthy on-location interviews with each television station, one after another, at the height of Gorbachev's visit. Boschwitz not only gained considerable free visibility in front of one of the state's largest-ever television audiences; the timing also served to remind everyone of the Governor's political motives. It made it easy for Boschwitz to put his spin on the proceedings.

Did reporters object to this media "manipulation"? On the contrary; they welcomed it! It was just what they needed, when they needed it. The only complaints were rumored to have come from members of the Governor's staff, because the ploy succeeded.

The point is that if you understand what a reporter needs and can figure out a way to provide it, you can dramatically improve your chances of getting coverage—for anything.

ONCE UPON A TIME...

A news story is supposed to be true, but otherwise the criteria for what makes a good story are the same as in fiction. We look for strong characters (newsmakers), good dialogue (soundbites/quotations), and something novel and dramatic to tell (scandal/disaster/victory). We strive to somehow touch our audience by relating things in personal terms, and we try to present it in a way that will attract and hold someone's attention.

If you hope to get your story told, you need to provide as many of those elements as possible. You should emphasize those things when you try to sell it to us. "News" is not something that's easy to define, but it's generally about significant events that affect people.

Picking the news of the day is a very subjective process. Reporters and editors routinely disagree among themselves about whether some story is truly newsworthy. We use fuzzy criteria like, "How many people does it affect?" But the answer can be, "Very few," and we may still call something a story. We cover fires and accidents all the time, which directly affect only a handful of people. And, some journalists argue that those things aren't really "news".

We're trying to put ourselves in the position of our viewers, listeners or readers. We try to gauge as best we can what is going to be interesting to them, or what we can do with a topic to make it interesting, to make it a "good story". That means when you argue that we should be covering something because it's a pressing issue, you may not be very persuasive. Instead, try giving us a personalized account, or some illustration that dramatizes your concerns.

PRESENTATION IS EVERYTHING.

I once happened to be in the office of one of my former news directors, when the station's weatherman stopped in. He wanted to know how the job search was going for another weather person for our staff. One of the questions the weatherman asked was, "Are we still looking for a meteorologist?" The news director carefully explained that the station still hoped to hire someone with those credentials, but he was having trouble finding a meteorologist who performed well enough on camera. The weatherman, who was both a meteorologist and a first rate on-air personality, asked, "Is presentation the most important thing?" He wondered if perhaps viewers cared more about the person's credibility and expertise, more about what the person had to say, than about the person's style. The news director's reply is a truth which all-too-often holds in television, "Presentation is everything."

Those are words to take to heart if you want to get media attention, especially television. Story ideas are killed every day in TV news rooms all over the country because, "It's a great newspaper story," which is another way of saying the story isn't visual. That's why protesters carry signs and sing songs and release balloons. They know that anything they can do for the cameras increases the likelihood that we'll tell their story. They might easily say what they want us to hear in a brief news conference. But they know that if that's all they do, chances are the story will get only a brief mention or not be told at all, because there's nothing to show people.

You're competing for air time with whatever else is happening that day. The best "presentation" often wins.

Non-News Conferences

News conferences are for stories that everyone already knows are newsworthy. They're one of the *least* effective ways to make a story newsworthy. The purpose of a news conference is to manage reporters, to set a time and place that's convenient for you and the media. You do it to avoid repeating the same thing over and over to each reporter who's interested. When police answer questions about a sensational crime, or politicians launch campaigns, they call news conferences. Often, what's said then becomes part of a larger story, with pictures of the crime scene, the campaign or whatever. When the news conference itself is all there is, then the coverage is often minimal, perhaps just one soundbite. Merely calling a new conference does not make the subject any more important. We may not come.

During my years as a government reporter, I've been to more worthless news conferences than I care to recall. I've seen the entire press corps berate public officials who plan to use us to attack their opponents. Instead we end up attacking whoever called us together, because there's so little justification for it.

Another recurring problem is length. There are times when an open mike draws politicians like moths to a flame (sometimes with the same fascinating result). No matter how brief the topic, everyone wants a turn. So they line up, spending half an hour or longer, plowing through prepared statements no one is likely to use. Sometimes a coalition of interest groups will hold a joint news conference to push their common agenda, and do the same thing. A radio colleague of mine coined a name for such exercises. He call's them "Last Supper" news conferences–an irreverent allusion that comes from the fact that a dozen people are lined up next to the podium.

Even a "solo" news conference can get cumbersome. Folks have a tendency to bring long prepared statements. It can get a little humorous. I've secretly laughed to myself more than once, when someone begins reading, then looks up and sees all the cameras simultaneously scatter around the room. As a look of consternation creeps across the person's face, I know they're wondering what in the world those photographers are doing. What they're doing is shooting cutaways, the wide views and other visual shots that will later help us to edit the story. It's video we need to get while the news conference is still happening. So the photographers shoot it when we're reasonably confident that you're not going to say anything quotable. That's almost certain to be when someone is reading. If we misjudge and you read something we like, we'll just ask you to repeat it, and it's likely to be more usable when you do.

Have a few brief statements prepared *in your head.* Take a few notes along for security. (If your statements are too long to remember that way, they're too long.) Then, be familiar with the topic and think about the key points you want to emphasize, so you can intelligently answer questions. If you have background information that you want reporters to have, put it in writing and hand out copies. If you have some legal boilerplate to get through, say it, but limit it as much as possible.

Experienced advocates are learning how to supplement news conferences with other more visual and personal elements. Instead of trotting out a spokesperson for "Welfare Mothers", a group might arrange for such a mother and her children, to appear and answer questions. Better yet, the group provides the names of some families we can reach at home, who we can interview and videotape that day.

If that sounds as though you're doing some of our work for us, you are. It's not that we're lazy. Most reporters prefer to do our own legwork, but there isn't always time. As you read this, there were hundreds of reporters who got to work this morning, were handed a news release, told to cover a morning news conference, find someone who's affected by whatever the topic is, and have a story ready to lead the early news. That's a lot to do in a matter of hours. In a small television market, it might be just one of two or three stories for that reporter to do that day. If we can't do the story visually within that time, the assignment editor will often decide not to cover it.

Obviously, the print media are less dependent on "visuals", but personalizing the story still helps. A story simply touting the latest statistics on tax increases may be easier to sell to a newspaper than to a television station. Still, a good illustration—like a widow about to lose her home because she can't afford the taxes—makes it a stronger story in any medium. Anything you can do to help us with your story increases the likelihood that we will tell it, and potentially increases the amount of coverage we'll give it. Would you rather see your story as a 10-second soundbite or a minute-and-a-half reporter's package? To fill that extra time, we need much more than quotations or a "talking head", and that requires more than a news conference.

Bring on the dog and pony.

Don't overlook the benefits of cheap theatrics. A clever presentation can make the difference between getting on the news and being ignored. An advocacy group known as the Minnesota Alliance for Progressive Action holds an annual rally at the State Capitol, which puts most other media come-ons to shame. MAPA, as it's called, is a coalition of labor and liberal social activist groups. It pushes for such things as higher taxes on the rich to fund services for the poor. At one of its rallies, three women dressed in black evening gowns and furs stepped out of a limousine in front of the capitol. They walked up the steps carrying signs with slogans such as, "Let them eat cake." Then, to complete the satire, they introduced themselves as, "Muffy, Buffy and Tuffy." For another year's rally, a "Cellular Phone Squad" appeared. It was a group of men dressed in suits and dark glasses, carrying portable phones, who fought to claim most of the pieces of a giant state "Budget Pie."

Such tactics are transparent attempts to attract cameras. They work, because it's a way to turn political abstractions into something visual. Good shtick tends to attract print reporters as well, if it's quotable and entertaining.

Compare that to the efforts of one of the group's political opponents. The Minnesota Business Partnership is a group of CEOs of major Minnesota companies. They also try to influence state policy, but their approach to the media has sometimes been conventional to an extreme. I've sat through news conferences that are painfully over-scripted, where some of the brightest, best paid executives in the state stand with their heads buried in press releases. They read carefully drafted statements that are so strained that one guy finishes by reading, "And - now - I'd - like - to - introduce - a - good - friend - of - mine..." and then the next guy begins, "Thank - you - Bob...," with his head still buried in a sheet of paper! (I'm not exaggerating.)

The Business Partnership has had its inspired moments (if you can ever call pandering to the cameras "inspired"). They once showed up in red baseball caps to talk about putting a "cap" on state spending. Hokey? Yes, and it didn't impress many lawmakers. But it got news coverage. The point is that when it comes to getting media attention, a face-off between the visual and the non-visual, or between the personal and the abstract, is no contest. The problem isn't that we'll ignore the views of either side. When budget issues come up, reporters frequently approach both groups for their opinions. But the purpose of a rally or news conference is presumably to *make* news, to immediately change the media's agenda.

Reporters are fickle, so it won't always work. The red cap campaign was panned by the newspapers. On a busy news day, we may dismiss you as "over-eager" and ignore you. (And we'll say to ourselves, "We don't cover mere media events.") But on a day when the news is slow, we may think your performance is a godsend.

It's like the proverb about the old prospector who bragged to another miner that he could make his mule do anything he wanted with just a simple command. When asked to prove it, the prospector agreed to a wager. Then, he promptly hit the animal on the side of the head with a two-by-four. Shocked by the brutality, the other miner exclaimed, "I thought you said you just had to speak to him!" Pointing to the mule, the prospector explained, "First you have to get his attention." Dealing with reporters can sometimes be like that. First you have to get our attention.

IT'S ALL RELATIVE

One of the questions that our friends and acquaintances sometimes ask us is, "What do you do for news on days when nothing's happening?" Many people have an image of news rooms where reporters sit around waiting for the phone to ring or for some fire alarm to sound. (It's an impression I confess I once shared.) Since everyone knows there aren't major fires or gruesome murders every day, folks reason that there must be days when nothing newsworthy occurs. That would be true if we used the same criteria every day to select stories, but we don't. What's news one day may not be the next.

When many things are happening, the threshold for what we consider to be a good story is much higher than on a day when things are quiet. At the height of the Persian Gulf War, it was hard to get any other news out at all. One night I found myself in the unlikely position of trying to convince a producer to let me do a story on the Governor's State of the State Address. The state's looming budget crisis had been making headlines for months, and the Governor would be outlining what he wanted to do about it. Normally, it would have been an obvious lead story, but now there was bigger news in the Middle East. The producer wanted to cut me back in favor of a late-breaking live report from Tel Aviv.

On another occasion, my boss rushed me more than a hundred miles by helicopter, to do a story about a small town. The news was that the town had too many cats roaming the streets. The first thing the Mayor said to me when I arrived was, "It must be a slow news day." He was right.

The Non-Story of a Career

If you've ever felt frustrated that the news media aren't more interested in your story, I can sympathize. I've never been reminded more vividly of the "relativity" of news than I was one summer during tornado season. I grew up in the Midwest's "tornado alley" and I've spent most of my career in places prone to such storms. But like most people, I'd never witnessed one. That is not until late one afternoon when we received word that a funnel cloud had been spotted in the Twin Cities' northern suburbs. We immediately dispatched every available crew and two microwave trucks (that we use to send back live reports) in that direction.

As a photographer and I headed that way, we saw the tornado. It was towering above the landscape like some malevolent spirit. The photographer leaped out and began videotaping it, capturing pictures we both knew were extremely rare. This was surely one of the great moments of our careers, we thought. We were seeing a tornado touch down, and we had it on tape!

As we followed it, I called in on the two-way radio,

"We have pictures of the tornado! Where's a live truck?!"

No response.

In just moments our 5 o'clock news would be on the air. I was frantic. I called again.

Still no response.

Our radio system wasn't the most reliable, so I thought perhaps no one was hearing me, or that I wasn't hearing them. Finally, someone on the assignment desk came on and directed us to a location where there had been damage on the ground. We were to go there and cover what had happened. A microwave truck would meet us there for a live report during the show. The voice added nonchalantly that we could send our videotape pictures from there.

I was mystified (and livid). The damage was clearly part of the story, but they were sending me to cover the sort of aftermath stuff we'd covered numerous times before. No one seemed interested in pictures of the tornado!

It wasn't until after I finished my report—without the tornado pictures (there was no time to send them)—and returned to the station that I discovered what had happened. The whole news room was ecstatic over our storm coverage, but it wasn't my work that thrilled them. It was something much more unusual than I could have imagined. When I was trying to radio in to tell them about our fabulous pictures, they and all of our viewers were watching live aerial pictures of the tornado from our helicopter.

"Sky 11" had already been in the air covering a downtown block party when the storm hit. The pilot Max Messmer and photographer Tom Empey had literally risked their lives to move close to the funnel and stay with it for several minutes. They sent back incredibly dramatic video of violent winds plucking trees like toothpicks and throwing them into sparking power lines. What they captured were the most definitive pictures ever taken of a tornado, and the first such video ever taken from the air. The images have since been studied extensively by the National Weather Service and other experts. Who cared about mere pictures from the ground?

No one was hurt and the storm did relatively little damage, but it was surely the most photographed tornado in history. It lingered on the northern edge of the metropolitan area for more than 20 minutes, as if to "pose" while hundreds of people took snapshots and home video. Thousands of people stood and watched it, some of them from the shoulders of highways where they pulled off the road in amazement.

What became of my photographer's pictures? The only time I ever used them was in a follow-up story I did that included photos and video taken by "ordinary" people. Even among those, our pictures were not the most dramatic.

Don't feel too badly if your story doesn't seem to be "selling". You're not alone. Selecting the news is a very subjective business, and nobody faces that reality more frequently than a reporter. It's one of our most common complaints. We all have stories we can't "sell" to our producers or editors, often for very murky reasons.

Hit 'em Where They Ain't.

Sometimes, as with the tornado, it all comes down to luck and circumstance. At other times, it's possible to predict when the news threshold will change. You improve your chances of getting coverage when that threshold is lowest. Experienced organizers often plan protests, announcements, and other events on weekends because Saturdays and Sundays are typically slow news days. It's a time when an event, which we might not even notice during the week, could turn into a major story–just to fill out a newscast. As an added bonus, the news on Sunday night is often the most heavily watched show of the week.

The first day of a legislative session tends to get heavy coverage. We show the opening gavel and review the pressing issues before the state. There are frequently rallies or protests over some of those issues, which we may cover. So, if you're organizing a demonstration at the capitol, opening day is a good time to do that, right? Wrong.

On a day when so much is happening, any one event can easily be lost in the shuffle. The amount of coverage it receives is almost certain to be restricted. There's only so much time in a newscast, only so many inches on a front page. I've seen an abortion rally, which drew hundreds of people, get only a brief mention among all the events the first day. It might have been the lead story, if organizers had held it just a day or two later. Better yet, they could have held it the day before, which was a Sunday.

Hook a Big One.

Another way to take advantage of the relativity of the news, is to latch onto some big story. Sometimes you can become a second report or "side bar" to a larger story. Maybe you have some expertise that can lend perspective to some world event.

In 1989 a Miami couple was shipwrecked in the Pacific Ocean when whales attacked and sunk their yacht. The pair, William and Simone Bulter, drifted in a rubber life raft for 66 days. Finally the Costa Rican Coast Guard rescued them, and their story immediately made national news. They had survived, they explained, because they had a special pump filtration system that created drinking water right from the ocean. The Butlers didn't mention that the pump was manufactured by a fledgling company called Recovery Engineering, but an executive with the company happened to hear early news accounts and immediately recognized his product.

A few phone calls later, the company president was flying to Miami to meet with the Butlers. Recovery Engineering was featured along with them in a Connie

Chung story on the *CBS Evening News*. Sales leaped 40%! The only calls that were more numerous than new orders were those from people interested in buying the business! To this day, whenever analysts discuss the now-publicly held company, they routinely mention the story of the Butlers and how Recovery Engineering's technology saved their lives.

Granted, your product may never save someone's life, but it doesn't have to. A competing company, WTC Industries, attracted publicity when it shipped water-filtering straws to the Saudi Arabian Navy during the Persian Gulf War. It was a great way for reporters to "localize" a story thousands of miles away. The war so dominated the news that for weeks almost nothing else could break into the headlines. (I know, I tried.) But by latching onto those events, a small company was able to attract media attention in a way that otherwise would have been impossible.

Sometimes, you can *create* a connection to a major story. Target stores loaded up a supply of bottled water off its store shelves in Minneapolis and shipped it to Milwaukee when the city's water supply was contaminated. The company repeated the exercise when a flooded Mississippi River forced the closure of the municipal water plant in Des Moines. Strohs Brewery used its bottling equipment to also send water to Des Moines. Both companies attracted publicity and built some good will for themselves, just by finding a way to "hook a big one". Try it, and you may find yourself "drowning" in publicity. (Sorry, I couldn't resist.)

"IF IT'S NEWS TO YOU, IT'S NEWS TO US."

An assignment editor I once worked under was fond of saying that—right after we'd missed something we should have covered. It was part of her job to be sure we were on top of things, but it wasn't always her fault when we weren't.

Don't forget to call us. It's often the people who most want and need news coverage who forget this most basic rule. When someone assumes a new leadership post in the Legislature, they frequently go through a little on-the-job training with the press corps. It can take a while for them to learn to warn us when they plan to do something newsworthy. All too often lawmakers make statements we know they'd love to see on the evening news, without making sure there will be any cameras present to capture them on tape.

It may be a group of members from the minority party, who storm out of a committee meeting en masse, protesting a decision they can't control. It may be a member criticizing the opposition from the floor of the state senate, complete with well-crafted soundbites. Such grandstand plays may make it into the newspaper, but it's almost worthless to the broadcast media. We don't have it on tape. There's nothing unseemly about notifying a reporter or two when you want coverage. The foolish thing is to set out to attract attention, and then do it when we're not there.

Occasionally, we get a call from a viewer who wants to know why we didn't cover some event. "There were all these people there," they tell us, "Why don't you care about...?" and so forth. More often than we like to admit, our answer is, "We didn't know about it." Sometimes I wonder if folks get so used to turning to the media for news that there's a tendency to assume that we're somehow omniscient. Of course we're not. As a rule, if you want a reporter to come, you need to ask one.

That typically means phoning an editor or someone on the assignment desk in a news room. When you call, ask to speak to whoever is in charge of planning stories, and make your "pitch" to that person. You can also contact a specific reporter who you think might be interested in your story. For example, if you're having trouble with some merchant, you might want to call someone who specializes in consumer stories. If you don't know who that is, again call your favorite news room and ask. In most news organizations, deciding what stories to cover is a collaborative process, among assignment editors, producers and reporters. Whenever possible you want to turn one or more of those people into an advocate for your issue or event.

Always put your proposal in writing. The big guys aren't the only ones who issue news releases. If your organization is holding a special fund-raiser and you want some publicity, put together a letter explaining what it's all about and where and when it will happen. Include the name and phone number of someone the reporter can reach to ask questions, and explain why you think it's newsworthy. You should send the news release out as much ahead of the event as possible. When it's received in the news room, we'll file it according to the day when the event will happen.

You may want to make one follow-up phone call to be sure we received the notice. That's also a good time to offer to answer any questions, but don't push. Even many media relations professions have trouble striking the proper balance between being "helpful" and becoming a "nuisance". Most stories live or die on their merits. How you design the event and when you hold it will have much more to do with whether we cover it, than any attempt at arm twisting.

It's usually not a good idea to demand to know whether we'll be there. It's not that we don't want you to know. It's just that on most stories, we don't make that decision until the day it happens. It will depend on what else is happening. (It's all relative.)

KNOW *YOUR* DEADLINE.

Every reporter has a deadline, and therefore so do you. If the story doesn't make it, the presses and the cameras can't wait, so it's "dead." (And sometimes so is the reporter.) I've already discussed the need to consider the deadline when you are responding to a reporter (chapter 4). When you're trying to sell a story, it's *critical*. If you want your story told, consider the reporter's deadline to be your deadline. Be sure to plan any event or announcement so there's enough time to get the story done.

As a rule, the safest time of day to do that is in the morning. That way, television reporters have plenty of time to write the story and get it edited for the evening news, and print reporters can file their stories for the next day's paper. The more in-depth you hope the story will be, the more time you should allow. Also consider how far reporters will need to travel. Is the story right in town, or a 2-hour drive away? You may also want to allow time for reporters to gather other information, if that will be necessary to do the story.

Sometimes you can target a particular newscast by the timing of an event. In many cities, the 10 PM show has the largest audience. But a story that has already appeared on an earlier show, may be shortened or dropped by ten (or eleven) o'clock. Holding your event or announcement until after the early news avoids that problem, but it also carries risks. News staffs are much smaller in the evening than during the day, so we may not have anyone to send.

You also guarantee that the earlier viewers won't see your story at all.

It's usually in your best interest to allow the reporter as much time as possible. The more rushed a story is, the greater the danger that something will be inaccurate or incomplete.

CONSIDER THE LOGISTICS.

There's an often-quoted saying in the military that, "Amateurs talk strategy; professionals talk logistics." It applies equally well to dealing with the media. For large news events like political conventions or national sporting events, the biggest single consideration is logistics. A tremendous amount of planning and expense goes into making sure that reporters have sufficient work space, phones, press credentials, etc.

Even for a much smaller event, you should try to anticipate what reporters will need. Let's say you've invited a noted speaker to address your organization's next luncheon and you want news coverage. Is there a place for reporters to sit and where cameras can shoot without blocking the view of your other guests?

It's ironic that television is the medium considered to be "instant communication" because a television story is by far the most cumbersome to prepare. In print or in radio, a reporter can collect much of the material for a story by phone. Once the information is gathered, a print reporter needs only to get the story written into a computer and it can go to press. In radio, a taped interview can usually be turned around within minutes and sent or received over a phone line.

The same story done for television requires much more—more people, more equipment, more time. It involves getting not only a reporter but also a camera person to the story. The gear we must transport includes the camera, tripod, microphones and lights, and it takes time to set up all that. A single story may require that our equipment be set up and taken down at several different locations.

Once the story has been "shot" it can still take hours or even days, before it's ready to go on the air. The reporter must review the videotapes, write a script, and record a "voice track". Then someone must electronically edit all of those things into a "package". That "package" is the reporter's story, which some anchor will introduce during a newscast.

A live report is even more cumbersome. It requires that a "live truck" and an engineer be sent on location. The reporter or a producer must arrange for a camera position, preferably within sight of something interesting and relevant to the story. We usually still need to shoot, write and edit a package to go into the live report. That package must then be "fed" by microwave or satellite back to the television station before the live shot begins. Some television stations don't have editing equipment in all live trucks. So the reporter's materials–the script, the videotape, and the voice track–must all be fed back to the station separately and edited by someone there.

All of that takes time. The less time a reporter has to do your story, the more likely it is that some part of it won't be told or won't be told as carefully as you would like. Just as the threshold for what makes a good story changes from day to day, the content of the story will change according to how much time is available to gather it. Deadlines can't be compromised, so stories sometimes are. There's a line news room wags sometimes use when stories barely make deadline, that makes the priorities clear:

"It's better than good. It's done."

TARGET THE MEDIUM.

Each medium has strengths and weaknesses, and your story may lend itself to one medium more than another. If you want to reach as many people as possible, quickly and with emotional impact, you probably want to play to the cameras. Television is good at portraying people–individuals with problems, feelings and concerns. TV also captures the spectacle of something such as a large rally or parade.

If on the other hand, you're trying to reach opinion leaders about a complex issue that would be difficult to treat adequately in just minutes, print might be more appropriate. A newspaper or magazine can devote more space to a story. Unlike broadcast news, the reader can go back over it if it's difficult to understand. Print reporters generally use more of the content of an interview within a story than television or radio, because their stories are longer.

The newspaper is also a good place to turn when the story involves past events, which have not already been covered. Television relies heavily on pictures. If there's no way to show what happened, the story is a much tougher sell. That's less of a problem in print. Some stories simply don't offer much in the way of "visuals", or the story demands a great deal of time and effort to get them. So again, the print media or radio may be an easier sell.

Sometimes the best way to target your message to a specific audience is through some magazine. Magazines have become extremely specialized, with very carefully defined readerships. There are publications on everything from body building to zoo management. Find one that matches the group you want to reach, and you may find that it's especially receptive to your story. The downside is that it may take weeks or months before the story is published. That's too long when you need to respond quickly.

Radio too has unique strengths. It's frequently the first to get a story on the air, sometimes within minutes. Talk radio is a format newsmakers often use to respond to allegations, because it's "live" and it allows for detailed answers. Public Radio has an audience composed of people who tend to have high levels of education and often incomes to match.

Some publications and television news magazines do entire stories that are really one long interview. *Playboy* and *Vanity Fair* feature articles that allow you to speak at length. Television journalists such as Barbara Walters do impressive work in longer formats. But those opportunities are rare, and normally reserved for celebrities and major public figures.

Give some thought to the audience you want to reach, and select the medium where you're most likely to find that audience. Then target that medium by calling the news outlet you want to use, and by making your story as appealing as possible—on that medium's terms.

COMPETITION IS YOUR FRIEND.

Competition can bring out the worst in reporters, but it can also be a useful tool to increase the coverage you get from us. During the '92 presidential race, I was sent to Dallas to cover a meeting between Ross Perot and his supporters. Before leaving, I mentioned my plans to some local Perot volunteers. They were having a rally in the Twin Cities, the night before the events in Dallas. One of my rivals, who covered the Minnesota event later told me that a Perot volunteer had tipped him about my plans. She had innocently asked, "Are you the reporter who's going to Dallas?" Of course he wasn't. He said his boss wouldn't let him go–until he found that I had gone. When he called his news director and explained that I was in Dallas, he had tickets on the first plane out the next morning.

The tip was accidental, but it certainly boosted the coverage Perot received.

BE THE ONE THAT GETS USED.

Would you like to see your company's name in public more, when the news is good? There are organizations that devote staggering amounts of money to promote their image, yet they overlook one of the simplest and most effective ways to draw attention to themselves.

How many companies spend thousands upon thousands of dollars to buy 30 seconds of time on the evening news? Even then, it's as a commercial without the subtle credibility a reporter or anchor might add within the context of a news story. There's a simple way to get news coverage, and it's almost certain to be favorable, neutral at worst. It doesn't require any special planning or strategy. It's usually quite passive. It works the same way for a school, a business or a public agency. All you have to do is say, "Yes," when a reporter calls, "Yes, you can take pictures of my employees working; Yes, you can talk to my customers; Yes, the reporter can videotape herself doing a 'standup' in my store."

You'd be amazed at the number of times reporters simply need a business or school or home of a particular type. We call it getting "generic" pictures or sound. Often it doesn't matter whose business it is. Maybe the story is about fast food wages. We don't care whether we show pictures in McDonald's or Wendy's. We just need someone flipping burgers. Reporters soon learn where we can do that, and where we can't. Most news rooms know of a nearby grocery store where they can quickly get pictures of food, or a liquor store when perhaps the story is about a tax on beer and wine. Those stories aren't about any particular store, but it's entirely possible that the store's logo may end up in the back of a shot somewhere, or on a price tag. It's free publicity.

Even if the story is negative–perhaps a recall of tainted beef–I know of a store where the manager will let me take pictures and I'll assure him that his store's name won't appear. I'll do that because the story isn't about him or his business anyway, and because I want him to let me come back. He knows that maybe next time he'll get a little free "air time".

The amazing thing to me is that so many organizations haven't caught onto this. Too often, I've asked a local business to allow us to take pictures, only to find that I must contact someone at the home office in Chicago or Los Angeles. After I spend the better part of an hour wading through the corporate bureaucracy, someone says they'll call me back. They do, but it's hours later, much too late for my deadline, and long after I've arranged to do the story somewhere else. Who do you think I'll call next time?

Some hometown companies have the same problem. When I was Business Editor, I used to do frequent stories about retail sales. At the time, there were two major retail chains based in the Twin Cities, Dayton Hudson and Donaldson's. Wanting to be fair, I would try to alternate between the two companies whenever I needed to go into a department store.

If I called Dayton Hudson, I usually received permission fairly quickly. If I called Donaldson's, I usually got the run-around. It wasn't that there was any controversy. The subjects were usually things like holiday shopping or the latest sales figures going up or down. They were the kinds of stories where you show people shopping. Guess where Twin Citians shopped in most of my stories?

Did that make any difference to the image of those companies? It's hard to say. Donaldson's doesn't exist as an independent business anymore. The point is if you want favorable coverage, be available and be convenient, or the reporter will simply go find someone else who is.

Conventional Wisdom

There are so-called "media experts" who disagree with me on this. Their argument goes something like this:

"A company may spend millions to cultivate a good public image. It has to be careful that one irresponsible reporter doesn't destroy that image overnight. It's just too risky to allow reporters in whenever they please."

Hence, many companies routinely turn down reporter's requests, or create vast bureaucracies for approving them. Let me explain why I think they're missing the point.

First, a single story–however bad–is no more likely to "destroy" a company's image than one commercial is likely to build it. Television and other media have a cumulative effect. They tend to leave impressions with people over time. That's why no one runs just one advertisement. Similarly, no one news report, good or bad, is the last word.

I'm not saying you don't need to be concerned about negative publicity. But if your company is in the habit of allowing reporters access, you're building up a base of good will over time, good will with reporters and with our audiences. That's precisely the kind of armor you need to protect yourself when a bad story comes along. Enough good publicity can outweigh the bad. Also realize that no negative story is likely to have any lasting effect unless it exposes a legitimate problem. When that happens, your biggest worry isn't the reporter.

Second, I'm not suggesting that you blindly do whatever any reporter wants. I'm saying you should cooperate whenever possible on those stories that appear to be harmless. I'm not telling you to voluntarily put your head on the block. As I've already discussed, there are many legitimate questions you should ask.

Favored Treatment

Some savvy newsmakers take this strategy one step further. They start thinking for the reporter. When they become aware of something newsworthy, they make it a point to tell one of us. This often happens between reporters who have a "beat" such as city hall, and the public officials who they cover. It doesn't have to be a "leak"–although we welcome those. It can simply be a cop who knows of a great crime story, or some controversial proposal sure to come up at the next council meeting. Officials who become reliable sources, can sometimes exact a price for their cooperation. They can occasionally ask that a reporter not use some piece of information, or request that a story be "held" for a while. A reporter will sometimes honor such requests to keep a reliable source. Besides, we're all human. Most of us tend to feel obligated to return favors. It doesn't take a mathematician to figure out how having a reporter indebted to you can be very helpful when a potentially negative story comes along.

UN-NEWS

Don't be too quick to decide that something you may have to say isn't "newsworthy". It doesn't always have to be new to be news. Some of the best stories explode popular myths, or reveal things that are known only to the experts in a particular field. Once when I was researching a story on pedophiles, I spoke with some investigators who referred me to organizations that openly advocate the legalization of sex with children. I'd read about the groups years before, and I didn't think mentioning them again would break any new ground. I changed my mind after talking to my bosses. "You mean these people claim to be lobbying state legislatures?!" they asked in disbelief. I realized that old information to me was very new information to them, so I included it in the piece. Just because you or the people in your field already know something, doesn't mean everyone else does.

The silliest things are sometimes newsworthy. Imagine making national headlines because of the way you tie your necktie. It happened to a Twin Cities news anchor. A viewer disliked the way the anchor's tie looked on the air, and showed up at the studio one night to teach him a different way to tie it. The anchor, Don Shelby of WCCO-TV, started using the technique and mentioned it to the clothier where he bought his suits. The shop owner asked if he could show the knot to other customers and Shelby agreed, not realizing what the owner intended. The next thing Shelby knew, the shop had mailed ads to a long customer list, and included a brief description of how to tie the *Shelby Knot*.

The Minneapolis newspaper picked up the story, partly to have a little fun at Shelby's expense, and partly because the technique appeared to be a truly new invention. From there the story continued to grow. Articles appeared in the *New York Times* and *People* magazine. Shelby, who I suspect was a little embarrassed at first, began having fun with the whole episode. He even demonstrated the technique on the air.

Here was a widely respected award-winning journalist getting the most attention of his career because of his tie. He was careful to credit the man who had shown him the technique, who said he invented it. Shelby even invited him onto the news set.

Article after article quoted men's fashion authorities saying they'd never seen the knot before. They couldn't find it in any of the "standard references". The Shelby Knot was the first advance in neck tying in decades, they proclaimed.

It wasn't at all. When the Minneapolis newspaper article first ran, it included a diagram of the knot. I was amazed to discover that it was how I'd been tying my tie since I was a boy. I learned it from my dad. He tells me he learned it from a booklet on tying ties when he was a young man. We had a good laugh over it. Shelby and some of the reporters who covered the story, began getting calls from others who were already familiar with the technique (a fairly elite club, apparently).

Does it matter whether the knot was truly new? Not really. It was new to Don Shelby, and to many other journalists. The reporters who covered it, had checked with the "experts" and it was new to them. It made a good story. Who knows, maybe the way you put your socks on in the morning will one day make you famous.

CHAPTER SEVEN:

THE INTERVIEW

The interview is the essence of what a reporter does. It's the primary way we gather information. But just as with sources, the image isn't always the same as reality. Strictly speaking, anytime you talk to a reporter, you're being "interviewed". It may be on the phone or in person, with or without a camera. When I call someone to arrange a "formal" interview, I may not even call it that. I'll just say that I'd like to come and talk to you. "Talk" in this context means I'd like to come to your home or office, with a photographer and a full complement of lights and microphones, and ask you some probing questions, the answers to which could end up on the six o'clock news— just "talk".

IT'S NOT, "JUST THE FACTS, MA'AM."

We want the facts, but what we're most likely to use is your *assessment* of those facts. When a reporter sits down to write a story, he or she will write a narrative, interspersed with quotations from sources. In television and radio, the narrative is what the reporter says. The quotations, as I'm sure you already know, are called "soundbites". Print reporters don't call them that, but anything that's true of soundbites, generally holds for quotations in print as well.

Let's say I've just come back from the scene of a fire. I'm about to write my story, and one of the things I have is a soundbite from a witness, which says:

> "I woke up when I heard the sirens, and when I looked out the window, my neighbor's house was on fire."

I have another soundbite with the same person, saying:

> "It looked horrible. With all that smoke and flames, it's a miracle anybody got out alive."

To a good reporter, the second quotation is unquestionably the better one to use. The first one is factual, but by the time I get to it in my story I've already said there was a fire. When I introduce the witness in my story, I will say she saw what happened. So the first soundbite will add little. The second one describes what the fire was like. It is an assessment of the situation from someone who was there. It helps to dramatize what happened.

It's not that the facts aren't important. My story will say where the fire happened, whether anyone was injured or killed, and so forth. Virtually all of those facts will come from sources who I've questioned. It's information that I'll include in the *narrative* part of the story. I'm trained to put those details together as clearly and succinctly as possible.

I use quotations to add "color" and perspective to the story. I don't need a legislator saying, "The state has a budget shortfall." I'd much rather quote him saying, "This is the worst fiscal crisis the state has ever faced." I don't need a homeless person saying, "I don't have any place to sleep tonight." Instead, I'll use the soundbite that says, "It's so cold out here, I'm afraid I might not make it until morning."

When the facts are enough.

There are exceptions, times when a statement of the bare facts is all that's needed. A witness to the fire may recount for me how someone rescued a small child from a bedroom window; the raw observations may be more compelling than any "assessment" she could add. I once covered a house fire that killed several kids. The family was in no shape to talk to reporters, but I located a cable television technician who just happened to be driving by shortly after the fire began. He had seen the smoke and tried to help. He broke down into tears as he explained to me how he heard children's screams and tried to get inside the house, but was driven back by the smoke and heat. He didn't have to say how awful he felt or assess for me how bad that fire was. It was written all over his face.

Sometimes a person will say something only he or she knows to be true, something the reporter can't confirm independently. A police investigator may release information about a crime; a politician may announce his re-election plans; an executive may say his company is about to complete a merger. Those kinds of factual statements will often run as is, perhaps followed by someone's assessment.

Feel free to editorialize—but with caution.

A reporter isn't supposed to express his or her personal opinions, but *you* can. That's frequently what a reporter wants you to do. We encourage you to be as outspoken as you like. Often, the more controversial you are, the better the story will be. When I'm covering some political dispute or public policy issue, my purpose is not to badger someone about their opinions. Rather I want you to, "Give me your best shot." If I can get everyone to do that, I can balance the story with opinions from all sides.

A reporter will try to avoid saying anything in the narrative of the story, which he or she can't personally confirm. We'll leave it to you to say those things that may not be so certain. That may mean we'll quote you saying whatever is the *least reliable* information in the story. In some stories, the reporter will then set out to refute what you say. Sometimes, we'll quote someone else who disagrees with you. In still other cases, we'll allow your statements to stand, carefully attributed to you.

If that sounds a little ominous, remember that you're the one who decides what you'll say. If you don't want it quoted, don't say it (Great Rule #1).

"How do you feel?"

When you hear that question, you're either dealing with a rookie reporter, or you've caught us in one of our weaker moments. The question, "How do you feel?" is an anathema to any good reporter. It's way *way* overused. To avoid that question, we may say something like, "You must be worried...," or ask, "How are you and your family coping with...?" or "What do you think should be done about...?" There are any number of ways to put it. But nonetheless, what we most frequently want to know is, "How do you feel?"

SETTING YOUR AGENDA.

A wise source never goes into an interview without some idea of what the desired result should be. If you're an advocate for some particular point of view, then you will want to concentrate on giving those facts and opinions that advance your cause. If you're an executive with some company, then you have a certain image and view to uphold, one that may not be your personal view. Depending on the story, you may need to defend yourself or your business.

Choose a few key points that you want to make. Then figure out how to express them succinctly. Ask yourself:

What do I want to be sure the reporter understands when the interview is over?

What information do I most want made public?

Are there stakeholders in this situation who expect or need to hear certain things from me?

Whenever possible, be prepared to provide concrete examples and data to support your assertions. Don't expect the reporter to simply take your word for what the facts are.

As I've already said, get as much information as you can from the reporter about what the story is and what the questions will be (chapters 3 and 4), but don't rely solely on that. You should try to anticipate what other questions we might ask. Presidents have their staffs draw up lists of potential questions before any news conference. Those professionals are good at anticipating what reporters want to know. You're probably not as skilled at making such predictions, but you don't need to be. You're not likely to face questions ranging from domestic policy to the future of the planet. If you know what the subject is, you should be able to make some educated guesses, and decide how you'll respond.

Be sure you know what you can and can't say (Great Rule #3). Go over in your mind how to express yourself without revealing anything you need to withhold. In most situations, you should be up front with a reporter about anything you're withholding: "Look, I want to talk to you, but I can't discuss details of the negotiations." That way, you turn a negative–the need to withold information, into a positive–a willingness to say as much as you can. Reporters don't always welcome such limits, but we're accustomed to them in many situations. As long as the restrictions are reasonable, most reporters will go along. We sometimes even preface our questions with something like, "I know you can't give me details, but can you explain the tone of the negotiations? Are you at least making progress?"

Occasionally, an aggressive reporter will press you anyway. So be prepared to justify any secrecy on camera, if it becomes necessary: "We just don't think it's productive to negotiate these issues in public, but I'll be happy to discuss them once we've resolved our differences."

Don't be too rigid. Media relations experts sometimes advise clients to stick to their pre-determined message, no matter what the reporter asks. That can lead to dodging questions, and other deceptions that can leave a negative impression with the reporter–and whoever sees the story. Remember, you want to appear open, not defensive.

The better prepared you are, the more relaxed and confident you'll be. It helps to have some political instincts, to anticipate how you might be misinterpreted. Then make it a point to be as clear as possible, wherever you think there might be any misunderstanding. Don't over-rehearse by trying to memorize your answers. That will sound as artificial to the reporter and the audience as it is awkward for you. Rather, try to have your major points in mind. Then explain yourself as you would to anyone in a conversation.

SETTING OUR AGENDA–THE PRE-INTERVIEW

Reporters working for different media, have different needs when they do interviews. A print reporter may not even ask to see you face to face. Often a telephone call is enough. A radio reporter frequently works by phone, using a tape recorder. In television, for obvious reasons, a phone call is almost never enough. We'll ask you to go on camera.

Most broadcast reporters like to do some sort of pre-interview. It's a technique that started in the days when television stories were shot on film. Because film was expensive and cumbersome to edit, reporters were expected to use as little of it as possible. So, a reporter would ask all the important questions before starting to film, and decide which answers were useful. Then, only those questions would be asked once the camera was rolling. Most of us now prefer not to do it that way. We've learned that the second time someone answers the same question, they're frequently less natural than they were the first time.

Instead, we use the pre-interview as a way to learn the facts of the situation. We get the basic who, what, when and so forth, which will go into the story's narrative. Often we'll do this on the phone before we meet with you. Sometimes we'll ask some background questions while the photographer is setting up the lights and tripod. Then, during the on-camera interview, we'll ask questions that will call on you to assess those facts. We may ask you what you think of the situation, how you feel about something, or what you plan to do now.

Some radio reporters work much the same way. It's simply easier to have those quotations that they might use, recorded on tape, and the other facts on paper. A print reporter will tend to intersperse both kinds of questions in a single interview. Still, the quotations most likely to be in the story, will be those that give your assessment. The reporter's ultimate choices are typically very similar to ones a broadcast reporter would make.

People often get these two kinds of interviews confused, and do exactly the opposite of what's needed. They're at their most quotable before the camera starts rolling, making all sorts of colorful analogies and concise observations–statements any reporter would love to have on tape. While the photographer is getting ready, a lawmaker may remark:

"Geez, this is a lousy way to pay our bills! The true cost will be in lost jobs!"

Then when the camera's rolling, folks suddenly feel compelled to give us every last detail. Their sentences get longer, as though they're afraid to leave anything out. That same thought becomes:

> "This tax proposal, which a small group of
> lawmakers announced today, is unnecessary and
> not in the best interests of all the hard-working
> people whom I represent. It will impact the economy
> in such a way that the businesses required to pay it,
> will be forced to cut back or close, and that will
> increase the unemployment rate."

The time for all those details is when you're explaining yourself to the reporter. It's important to do that. The reporter's grasp of your ideas and opinions is crucial to how we tell the story. But when the tape is rolling, your audience is no longer the reporter. It's the viewer or listener. The time you have to make your case is dramatically shorter. You're bound by the same constraints the reporter faces when the interview must be edited into a story. You should be trying to convey the essence of your thoughts, as briefly and creatively as you can.

LIVE VS. TAPED–TWO DIFFERENT APPROACHES

In broadcast news, there are important differences between a "live" interview, and one that's recorded. The two are different in how the reporter handles them, and you should handle them differently too. In a taped interview, the *reporter* decides what answers will be part of the story. In a live interview, *you* decide.

When It's Recorded

Reporters can take great liberties when we know that whatever happens can be edited later. We don't have to let anyone hear our questions. We can take as long as necessary to get the answers we want. If someone I'm interviewing is being evasive, or if they simply have trouble being concise, I may ask the same question more than once. I'll rephrase it, or I may simply ask someone to restate what they've told me. I can afford to be very casual, even rambling. I sometimes ask very open-ended questions with no obvious answer, just to see where it may lead. If it goes nowhere, what have I lost? Just a few feet of videotape.

Taped interviews are usually cordial, but not always. The reporter can be rude or aggressive, even to the point of trying to provoke you, and never show that to the viewer. Investigative reporters will sometimes do very long interviews, attempting to wear down a source. The techniques they sometimes use are similar to those used by a police interrogator. The approach can range from gentle cajoling to outright badgering.

It's *what* you say that's important, not *how much*. A television crew typically shoots about 20 times more videotape than will ever be put on the air. For an in-depth story, the crew may shoot a hundred times as much. We may use only one or two pieces, and we choose which ones. You need to be sure you're comfortable with anything we might pick.

When It's Live

Most people are more intimidated by live interviews than by those done on tape. They're afraid that they'll say something wrong, and it won't be possible to correct it.

They don't realize that a live interview offers some advantages. It can be a great equalizer between you and the reporter or anchor. I know of occasions when public figures who are accustomed to dealing with the media have insisted they will only do an interview that is live. They know that it forces the reporter or anchor to behave.

First, there's a time limit, usually only a few minutes. That means all questions must be to the point. When there's only time to ask three or four questions, no one is going to do much experimenting. In many situations, that makes it easier for you to predict what we'll ask you. Second, the viewers see everything: the questions and the answers. That means there's no risk of anything being taken out of context. It also means the viewers see how the reporter/anchor treats you. If he or she wants to badger you, it will have to be done where everyone can see. That usually means we'll be cordial.

When a reporter conducts a live interview, we're trying to be a surrogate for the viewer. If that's done well, then the viewer will tend to identify with the reporter, and may or may not sympathize with the person being interviewed. A skilled interviewer can even direct the audience's sympathies to some extent. But if the reporter isn't careful, the viewer's loyalty can quickly shift. During the 1988 presidential campaign, Dan Rather did a live interview with then-Vice President George Bush. The main topic was the Iran-contra scandal, and Bush's alleged involvement in it. Rather, who has a well-earned reputation as an aggressive reporter, went on the attack. He repeatedly pressed Bush to concede that he knew more than he was admitting. Bush refused to back down, and the conversation became very heated.

Perhaps, that's what Rather intended. It certainly promoted his intrepid image. However, the impression it gave many of those watching was that Rather was "going after" a presidential candidate. There was considerable criticism of Rather's tactics, even from other journalists. As for Bush, the exchange not only failed to hurt his election chances, it may have helped. In the eyes of some, he demonstrated that he was a forceful leader, someone who's not easily intimidated.

During the '92 presidential race, candidates Ross Perot and Bill Clinton used live formats extensively. Perot appeared on Larry King. Clinton was fond of doing local radio call-in shows. The pundits called it a "revolutionary" way to prevent network reporters from filtering the candidates' messages–the revolutionary "live interview".

Impressions Count.

A live interview is a lot like meeting someone for the first time. Unless you're a very famous person, you're being "introduced" to thousands or even millions of viewers or listeners. So if you want to make a favorable impression, you should be on your best behavior. Just as a reporter or anchor can lose sympathy by appearing to be too aggressive, so can you. Most viewers are taken back by an interviewer who is rude or abusive, and they'll react the same way if you are. You want to give the impression that you are forthcoming, not defensive, that you are trying to provide information, rather than hide it.

Indeed, volunteering new information is an excellent tactic to use with a tough interviewer. If you can provide facts to support your case, which the reporter may not already know, then it's the reporter who may have to do some quick thinking. A clever newsmaker can be very disarming.

On live television, you have to be conscious of your appearance. That means tasteful make-up for women. For men it means a fresh shave or neatly trimmed beard. It means clean and well-combed hair, and no food between your teeth. Your clothes will vary according to the circumstances, but should be appropriate to the image you want to convey.

You don't want to look as if you're made out of plastic, but anything about your appearance that attracts attention, will inevitably detract from what you have to say. As any news anchor will tell you, viewers tend to focus on how you look. (A new haircut attracts far more calls from viewers than most stories.)

Unless the topic is tragic, smile, even on radio. You'll sound more pleasant. Believe it or not, you can "hear" a smile.

Note: Live on Tape

There's a hybrid format that you may run into, if you ever do a talk show. It's called "live on tape". What that means is that the show or the interview is recorded in real time, to be aired later, with little or no editing. For all practical purposes, it's still a live interview and you should approach it as one.

The only difference is that if you try to surprise us and moon millions of viewers, we can take that part out.

Then again, we may not.

BEING QUOTABLE

Remember when your English teacher told you, "A single sentence contains one complete thought." She didn't realize it at the time, but she was talking about a television soundbite. Soundbites average around 10 seconds in length. That's about one long sentence or two short ones. You may have the most brilliant observation of your life to make, but if it runs much longer than that, chances are only part of it will make it into the story. That's not to say that we'll use your words out of context. We may paraphrase the rest, but that's at the discretion of the reporter.

A well-delivered quotation is a tool you can use to draw attention to yourself, or to help direct the way we'll use you in the story. It can work well in any medium, but it's definitely true in television, where time constraints put a premium on a well-turned phrase.

There's an amazing degree of unanimity among reporters about what makes a good soundbite. When covering the same news conference or interview, we frequently pick exactly the same quotations. At the 1988 Democratic Presidential Debate in Des Moines, part of the format was for each of the contenders to ask questions of one other candidate. A lottery determined who questioned whom, and former Arizona Governor Bruce Babbitt drew the name of then-Tennessee Senator Al Gore. Gore had suspended his campaign in Iowa, as part of what would turn out to be an ill-conceived "southern strategy". He had already faced criticism for ducking the battle. Babbit turned to Gore and casually said,

"Al, it's good to see you back. You know I thought they might start putting your picture on milk cartons."

The line got a big laugh and ended up as part of my report.

I wasn't the only one who picked that bite. I was sharing a satellite truck and other facilities with several other reporters. We filed our reports for cities scattered all across the country, each of us appealing to different local audiences, with different demographics and different political concerns. When we talked about it later, we discovered that out of the entire debate, every one of us had used the "milk carton" soundbite.

Our collective "bias" didn't favor any particular political view or candidate or favored issue. We just knew a good quotation when we heard one.

Experienced sources learn to pick up on what we want. During one of the daily Washington briefings on the Persian Gulf War, then-Pentagon Spokesman Pete Williams was asked, "Can you give us a brief summary of the current situation?" Williams had already spoken in considerable detail about exactly what was happening, but he knew that wasn't what the reporter meant. Without even a pause, he replied, "I think I sense a television soundbite coming." Then, after the press corps' laughter subsided, he delivered one.

If you can capture the essence of your ideas in a brief articulate statement, you can sometimes "feed" a reporter a certain soundbite, one we're almost certain to use. It's a way to highlight some point you want to make, to increase the chance that we'll include it in the story. A good soundbite will also make your main point more memorable to whoever sees or hears it.

Modern politicians have raised the crafting of good soundbites to an art form. It's rare for any experienced public official to deliver a speech without including at least one or two of these zingers. Before an interview, they often dream up carefully worded answers to questions they know a reporter will ask. They may use the same key sentence in interviews with several different reporters. (We don't usually mind. I'd be more upset if a competitor got a better soundbite than I did.) Rather than object to such practices, reporters tend to criticize the official who isn't "savvy enough" to give us something we can use.

There are times when we go trolling for soundbites. When we need reaction to something from several different sources and time is limited, we may interview someone only long enough to get what we need and move on. With some people that can take quite a while. With others, it's the answer to our first question. Give us one good quotation, thank you, and the interview is over.

It's ironic that television takes so much criticism for supposedly minimizing or "soundbiting" what people say. Soundbites drive the way a reporter writes a typical broadcast story. In some cases they can even overshadow the video, which in television is no small feat. It's as though what we write is the mortar that holds the story together, and the soundbites are the bricks. The first thing we do after "shooting" a story is transcribe the soundbites. Then we fit the rest of the material around them. What you say to us, can and does change the way we tell our stories. There are times when a soundbite can direct a story as surely as a rudder steers a ship.

The Art of Soundbiting

There's something odd about speaking "television". Some people come by it naturally, while others never seem to get it at all. When Minnesota began lengthy legislative hearings and debate on what would become landmark Health Care Reform Legislation, the plan had several key architects among lawmakers. Representative Paul Ogren led the charge in the House, while Senator Linda Berglin was the point-person in the Senate. Another key player was then-Senate Minority Leader Duane Benson.

Ogren and Benson were what reporters call soundbite machines. The challenge with them wasn't getting a soundbite. It was picking one from so much good material. Between them, the two men represented both legislative chambers and both parties–a perfect balance. So they tended to dominate the news coverage on the issue.

Berglin, however is one of the least quotable people I've ever tried to cover. She's an exceedingly bright and dedicated woman, but she just doesn't speak the language.

The media favoritism towards Ogren and Benson became so obvious that some of Berglin's colleagues began to complain to the Capitol Press Corps. "Why were we ignoring someone who was working so hard on a major issue?" they asked. The answer was we weren't ignoring her at all. We were well aware of the lack of credit she was getting, and some of us had tried to include her. Unfortunately, we had very little to work with. She could speak on the Senate floor for the better part of an hour, without once uttering a usable quotation. The problem wasn't following her thoughts. She was perfectly understandable. But her sentences were too long, her grammar too complex, her delivery too mundane. Her words were like a videotape that's been re-recorded so often that the picture has faded into electronic "snow". Eventually, some editor looks at it and says, "It's just not broadcast quality," and out it goes.

I know that's a harsh assessment, but it's one reporters make all the time. Part of our job is to keep stories lively and interesting. Politicians are understandably concerned about who gets credit for things, as they should be. But that's not always at the top of a reporter's list of priorities. It's not with our viewers either. I need to tell them what happened on an issue, not necessarily who did what behind the scenes. Berglin did occasionally get coverage, but in a setting like the Legislature, there are always plenty of people clamoring for our attention. Like it or not, the best soundbite often wins.

What makes a good soundbite? Here's a quick list of criteria:

It Must Be Brief.

You already knew that, right? It's one of the great criticisms of television, that we never let people finish speaking. No one points that out any more gleefully than our print colleagues, but pick up a newspaper sometime and look at the quotations. Read a few of them out loud. You won't find many that take more than 10 seconds to say. In most newspapers you'll find mere phrases quoted, even single words. If you count the quotations as a percentage of the total written copy, the ratio is much smaller than in television. Surprised? You shouldn't be. Journalists considered brevity a virtue long before television was invented.

Television isn't above a little creative editing either, but imagine the uproar if *we* started routinely cutting people off in mid-sentence, or quoting only a single word! The perception is different in print, but the reality is much the same. In any medium, if you want to be quoted, be brief. There's very little you can say about a television soundbite that isn't also true in print.

Talk About What You Know.

Always speak in first person. Whether you're a victim of a crime or a candidate for the Senate, talk about what you know to be true. The primary reason a reporter interviews anyone is to learn about things that you've personally witnessed, experienced or decided.

Give Your Assessment.

As I discussed before, your opinions count—sometimes more than the facts.

KISS: Keep It Simple, Stupid.

Whoever first coined that phrase, wasn't referring to soundbites, but it fits. You need to speak in short declarative sentences. The soundbites that are the most difficult to use are like this sentence; they run on and on (and include brief asides, which the speaker thinks will help to clarify what's being said) before they finally get to what may be a good point, but I can't use it because by then it's too long and I can't separate the good stuff from all the garbage in the middle. (Pant! Pant!)

I think some people are afraid that all their wonderful insights will be lost if they can't somehow cram them all into a single sentence. It's usually a futile exercise. What happens is, instead of getting all those ideas into the story, you simply force the reporter to choose a different quotation.

It Helps to Use Analogies, or Humor.

In a story I once did on how Minnesota Governor Arne Carlson was faring in office, I interviewed a lobbyist and political analyst named D.J. Leary. D.J. is a popular guest with reporters looking for some good political commentary, because he knows the terrain and he's so quotable.

The Governor had had a rocky first year in office. His lowest point came when his staff failed to return vetoed bills to the Legislature before the constitutional deadline. So the legislation became law despite the Governor's highly publicized objections. Unfortunately for Carlson, it wasn't just one bill. It was a whole stack of them.

D.J. noted how incompetent the oversight made the administration look and how Carlson, a former state auditor, had run as someone who, "Knew how to get things done." Instead, in DJ's words, "He looked like a guy who sits down at a poker table and asks, 'How much are the pictures worth?'" I had my soundbite. It was a wonderful analogy, with the added benefit that it was funny.

D.J. is in good company. Ronald Reagan is famous for his one-liners. So are other politicians (e.g., Bruce Babbitt), and for good reason. Of all types of jokes, one-liners most easily fit into a news story. The secret is to be both funny *and* brief. Otherwise, no matter how clever you are, there isn't enough time to hear it.

It Helps to Use Rhetorical Devices.

Sometimes, you want to set the statement apart from ordinary spoken English. The most famous example of this technique happened more than 20 years ago. Columnists and commentators had been asserting for years that there was "an eastern liberal establishment", when then-Vice President Spiro Agnew referred to it as a bunch of "effete snobs" and "nattering nabobs of negativism." He was quoted everywhere. (The alliteration has since been credited to his speech writer William Safire.) In recent years, I've heard Agnew credited with having *begun* the onslaught of attacks on the "liberal media". He wasn't the first to use such labels. But the fact that some people now perceive that he started it all, is testimony to the power of a good soundbite.

Avoid Jargon and Clichés.

Every profession has its jargon and technical terms, including mine. I have to sometimes remind myself that terms like "S-O-T" (sound-on-tape) and "NATS" (natural sound) don't mean anything to most people outside television news. If you're a doctor who's just treated an accident victim, don't say, "She suffered lacerations and contusions;" say, "She has cuts and bruises." If you're an engineer, say, "cool off," not, "dispel excess heat energy."

Sometimes a brief definition is a good substitute for jargon. Instead of saying, "He's HIV positive," say, "Blood tests show that he carries the AIDS virus." You may want to speak in terms of effects. If you're a union advocate, don't say, "The company wants to 'eliminate seniority'." Say, "If we agree to this contract, any of us could still lose our jobs, no matter how long we've worked here."

When it comes to clichés, sports figures are by far the worst offenders (including sports reporters). How often have you heard, "We have to take them one game at a time," or "They're a very physical team."? (Does anyone play two games at once against spiritual opponents?). In all fairness, when you talk about the same subject over and over, as often as athletes do, it's tough to find fresh ways to say the same things. It's a problem that plagues some kinds of news stories. How many times have you heard the neighbor of some crime victim say, "I never thought this would happen here."? You'll make yourself much more quotable when you can put things into your own words, rather than repeating phrases you've heard before.

The scariest thing about giving a reporter a cliché is not that we'll cut you out of the story. It's that we'll use it.

Be Natural.

Please don't think it's always necessary to craft soundbites before you talk to a reporter. Often just taking a few minutes to collect your thoughts is enough. A good interviewer is skilled at helping you articulate your ideas, and getting the needed quotations from you naturally. The preferred style for journalism these days is conversational. Most people do just fine by simply talking.

That means, don't become too preoccupied with grammar and sentence structure. *Relax.* Senator Berglin was competing for attention with 200 other politicians. You're probably not going to be. In most situations the reporter will edit out your "ums" and "ahhs". It's not that you should always count on us to make you look good; it's just that anything that isn't to the point, eats up precious time and space. We can't afford to let you ramble.

One of the most compelling moments in television in years came during the 1992 riots in South Los Angeles, when beating victim Rodney King appealed for calm. If anyone had a right to be outraged, it was the man who police had beaten. The acquittals of the officers involved was incomprehensible to many who had seen the attack on videotape. But in the midst of that chaos, King's voice was one of sanity. I'm sure he made English teachers everywhere cringe. His phrasing wasn't remotely grammatical. His statement, which lasted some two minutes, was much too long by television standards, but it ran at the top of the evening news, in its entirety. Why? Because it was so timely and so genuine. He broke nearly every rule for what makes a good soundbite, except the most important one: *Be yourself and be candid.* I know that sounds a little corny–like your old English teacher talking again–but it's true and it works.

For most people, speaking television or radio is like learning to swim or play the violin. It takes training and practice, and perhaps some innate talent not everyone has. You may never be a soundbite machine, but with a little effort you can at least learn a simple rendition of "Do Re Mi."

ACCEPT COACHING NOT PROMPTING

If you're not accustomed to doing on-camera interviews, the reporter or producer will gladly help you. When the person doing the interview is there with you, you should look at him or her, not the camera. As much as possible, you should pretend that the camera isn't even there. Just hold a conversation.

In some situations, we may ask you to talk to us from some remote location. That location could be a television studio, or perhaps your living room. You then talk to the anchor or reporter "through" the camera, so you should look right into it. You'll be able to hear the questions through an ear piece that we'll give you.

Beware of the reporter who starts telling you what you should say. Some inexperienced reporters will ask you to, "Please say it like this..." They're usually trying to get you to condense your thoughts down into one usable soundbite, but sometimes the motive is more sinister. Be sure that whatever is being suggested is truly your thoughts, and then put it into your words. Don't let someone over-dramatize your thoughts, by persuading you to say, "So-and-so is a jerk!" when all you really intended to say was that you disagree with something so-and-so did.

KNOW WHEN TO STOP.

Don't keep talking just to fill time. Sometimes a reporter will wait to follow up on a brief answer, hoping that you'll embellish it. Most people feel uncomfortable when there's silence in a conversation. So, the interviewee will often begin to ramble, saying more than intended. When you're comfortable with the answer you've given, stop. Let the reporter fill the silence. A prolonged pause isn't likely to be used in the story unless it shows your obvious discomfort, or reveals that you're refusing to answer. If you feel the stare of the camera, concentrate on looking eager to answer the *next* question.

IT AIN'T OVER TILL IT'S OVER.

Many people who are otherwise skilled at handling interviews, tend to let their guard down whenever they think the camera has stopped rolling. It's understandable for anyone who gets nervous in front of a TV camera, which is nearly everyone. Some reporters take advantage of this phenomenon by having the photographer 'pretend' to stop. The reporter may say. "Thank you," or compliment you on doing a good interview–something that implies that the interview is over without saying so. The photographer then steps away from the camera, adjusts a light, or starts moving cables in a way that makes it appear that the shooting is over, but the camera is left on.

Someone who is tense during an interview, will often become more natural at that point, even though the reporter is still asking questions. The result can be an excellent soundbite that it was impossible to get before. Since most of us prefer to look natural rather than uptight, you may be just as pleased with the results of such a ploy as the reporter. However, it's also a time when something may slip out that you would prefer not to have on videotape.

Clever sources keep careful track of whether the cameras are rolling. Once during difficult negotiations over tax reform, the governor arranged to meet with legislative leaders, but then sent a staff person. The house speaker was a little miffed and said so to reporters–diplomatically. After the impromptu interview ended, she remarked,

"We want to talk to the organ grinder, not the monkey."

"We weren't rolling on that!" we all moaned in unison.

"I know."

PRACTICE.

Interviewing is a skill, and so is being interviewed. Just as reporters get better with experience, so can you. If you're someone who has occasion to talk to reporters from time to time, approach each encounter as a practice session, a way to hone your skills. Look at the story as a way to get a better sense of how you express yourself. Note which of your statements we tend to use, and try to understand why. Whenever possible, record yourself on your VCR, and use it to evaluate your "performance". As with any skill, you'll find that you get better at it the more you do it.

* * *

Once you've said something, you can't take it back (Great Rule #1), but you can sometimes ask the reporter not to use it. If you misspeak during an interview, stop and say so. Ask if you can restate your thoughts. Most reporters will agree unless they suspect that there's some deception.

Sometimes you can later add to what you've said. If you find new information before the reporter's deadline, call us with it. You can even offer new quotations to a print reporter. Maybe you later think of a clever way to say something. The reporter might use it, if there's time to and still finish the story by deadline.

Finally, keep in mind, that the interview is part of a larger context. If you have other supporting data, background information or statistics, provide them in writing if possible. You may want to give the reporter a "press packet" containing relevant information and pictures. Print reporters usually require more detailed information than broadcasters, but anything that supports the points you want to make is always worthwhile.

Life is far more complex than soundbites or quotations. You can't hope to fully explain yourself using them. You can, however, explain yourself to the reporter before, during and after the interview. It's that explanation that often determines your role in the story, not just what soundbites you deliver.

CHAPTER EIGHT:
CONFIDENTIAL SOURCES AND OTHER RESTRICTIONS

Demanding to stay anonymous, or insisting that a reporter can't use certain information, is the most direct way that a source can control a story. It puts you in the position of telling us what we can write or say. That's considerable control. It's control most reporters do not like giving you. But we recognize that at times it's necessary. We know there are situations in which a story could threaten a job, a personal relationship, or even someone's life if we reveal that person's identity. Without the use of anonymous sources, some stories would never be told.

A popular misconception of reporters is that we're constantly seeking out secret sources, and using unnamed people to get our stories. In reality, the vast majority of stories don't involve anonymous sources. It's not necessary. I'll grant you that some reporters are fascinated with the perceived mystique of anonymous sources and silhouette interviews, and may use them when it isn't necessary. But most of us avoid such restrictions whenever we can. Unnamed sources tend to raise questions about how reliable the story is–and how reliable the reporter is–so we use them sparingly. A story is always more credible if we can say where we got the information.

Reporters justify using unnamed sources because we like the story; we don't decide to do the story because it has unnamed sources. Keeping someone anonymous or information "off the record" is nearly always something done at the request of the *source*, not the reporter. It's done to protect *you* so we can gather information you wouldn't otherwise give us. It's an arrangement a reporter settles for because it's sometimes the only way for us to tell the story. *You need to convince the reporter that the restrictions are necessary.*

Having said that, let me admit that reporters see a promise of confidentiality as a powerful way to leverage information. We also know that any risk *we* take when we give that promise, is usually quite small compared to the one *you* take when you accept that promise. Be suspicious of any reporter who seems overly eager to promise you confidentiality. You have the most to lose if the agreement is in any way ambiguous, misunderstood or deliberately abused. You're the one who needs to be sure everything is carefully arranged *before* we tell the story.

JOURNALISTIC TRADITION

Some reporters feel so strongly about a promise of confidentiality, that they would go to jail rather than reveal such a source. A journalism professor of mine once said a reporter's pledge to keep a source confidential must be absolute. He sternly lectured us on the damage we would do, not only to our credibility, but also to the whole journalism profession, if we ever broke such a pledge. His reasoning is obvious: If anonymous sources can't count on a reporter to protect them, then soon there won't be any anonymous sources.

Not everyone has the same respect for such agreements. The courts have never fully recognized a reporter's right to protect sources. Such agreements do not have the same status under the law as say an attorney/client or doctor/patient relationship. It's difficult for either reporters or sources to know what a court might do in a given situation.

Not all news organizations consider such agreements unbreakable. Some news rooms have written policies saying, when it comes to confidential sources, they will "obey the law." That's a nice way of saying that if a judge orders them to reveal your name, they will. Many reporters strongly disagree with such policies, but it's a rare individual who's capable of fighting the court and the boss at the same time. On the other hand, I should point out that reporters deal with confidential sources all the time, and it's rare for anyone to contest such agreements in court,

The cynics would have you believe that there's no such thing as "off the record", no truly anonymous sources. They're convinced that reporters have no qualms about betraying a source when it suits our purposes. With some reporters that's true, but most of us feel obligated to protect such relationships, if only out of enlightened self-interest. We know that a reliable secret source can lead us to excellent stories, stories no other reporter may be able to duplicate.

DEFINE TERMS.

In a confidential conversation with a reporter, it's *critical* that you define terms. The phrases reporters and sources use are sometimes defined differently by different people. You don't want to find out later that what you meant by "off the record" is not exactly the same thing the reporter meant by "off the record."

Let me give you the definitions I use, and which I think most *(but not all)* reporters use. Always, be sure you get a specific explanation of what the reporter intends to do. Don't accept some vague assurances couched in jargon. In this kind of relationship, the reporter is holding most of the cards. His or her primary interest is telling a story, with as much credibility as possible. You're the one who's at risk if someone identifies you, or uses information you want withheld. An unscrupulous reporter may be counting on keeping things ambiguous. That way, if you later object to the story, the reporter can claim that there was just a "misunderstanding."

Above all, *make sure the reporter agrees to your terms before you provide the information.* As long as you possess the information, you control what's done with it. Once the reporter has the information, the reporter is in control.

"Off the Record"

This is as restrictive as you can get. It means that nothing that you say will be repeated, anywhere, anytime. It enters the reporter's ears and stops. Period. The information normally is one piece of a larger story. (If it was the whole story, what would be the point of telling it?) It may be something needed to clarify other facts. It may be information offered to refute something. It may be something a source says to gain a reporter's confidence, to convince the reporter that the source knows what he's talking about. Sources ask to go "off the record" to give information that they hope will influence a story, or perhaps kill it altogether. But above all, whatever is "off the record" cannot be included.

This restriction is used by people who are trying to defend their own actions, the actions of their organization, or the actions of someone they represent. I've dealt with attorneys who've asked to go "off the record" to try to defend their client without publicly revealing their case. I've had people ask to go "off the record" to tell me something very personal or unflattering about someone in my story. They want to be sure I understand who I'm dealing with, but don't want me to use the information.

Government officials sometimes go "off the record" to be sure that a reporter understands the context of something. They may feel that a story will be more damaging if they don't somehow justify their actions. Sometimes an official feels reporters can only fully understand policy decisions if we have information that can't be published because of political or security considerations. By going "off the record" a source may hope to convince us that a seemingly foolish decision was indeed wise, but for reasons that can't be made public.

As I've already emphasized, you should get the reporter to agree to your restrictions in advance. But occasionally a source asks us to keep something "off the record" by withholding information we already have. For example, police may ask us not to reveal that they are seeking a particular suspect, because if we name him, that person might flee. Some reporters will agree to such requests. Others make it a practice to use whatever information they have and, "Let the chips fall where they may."

Our decision often depends on what the information is. If it's major stuff and there's any reason to suspect that a competing reporter may also have it, there's a much greater temptation to go with those facts. If only one reporter has the information, it's sometimes easier to convince him or her to hold it. Few reporters are eager to bear the blame for torpedoing an investigation, if you can convince us that's what the story would do.

Sometimes images are the issue. Authorities sometimes ask us not to show the faces of undercover officers who may be at the scene of a crime, and we normally agree.

The inherent problem with any request made after the fact is that you're simply appealing to the reporter's good will (which is always risky). It's a gambit. By even raising the issue, you're confirming that the information in question is true, and reporter has no obligation to do what you ask. Still, if the reporter has facts that you don't want revealed, such a request may be your last hope. We will sometimes agree to your request.

"Not to be Used From This Source"

This is a variation of "off the record." It's a distinction that we make to protect ourselves. It means that we agree not to use the information you provide, *unless* we can obtain that information from some other source. If that happens, the reporter is free to include it in the story. It's a safeguard to prevent a reporter from being duped into withholding information that might become public anyway. A cunning source might reveal incriminating information "off the record", knowing that the reporter could learn about it anyway. That might then co-opt the reporter into keeping it a secret.

Let's suppose a reporter hears a rumor of an imminent tax increase. A city official then agrees to talk "off the record" and says a budget shortfall will soon force a major tax hike–but the source doesn't want that made public until after the upcoming election. A reporter who accepts that restriction is agreeing to help deceive the public! Breaking the "off the record" agreement may be unethical, but so is keeping it. The best way out of the dilemma is to try to confirm the information some other way, and that's exactly what any self-respecting reporter will do.

Many reporters argue that this kind of out clause is automatically part of any "off the record" agreement, but they don't always tell you that.

"Not for Attribution"

This is the classic "anonymous source" agreement. It means the reporter can use the information, but won't say where it came from. It's used by people who want the information included in the story, but who doesn't want it attributed to them. Such sources do not lurk around in dark alleys wearing trench coats. They're typically "whistle blowers" and other people who are critical of some person, organization or decision–but who feel they can't say so openly.

There are different degrees of anonymity under such agreements. The purest form is when you hear a statement like, "NBC News has learned..." It says nothing at all about where the reporter got the information. Reporters are sometimes willing to do this when they can confirm the same information with more than one person, or when we consider the source very reliable. Perhaps it's a source the reporter has used before, or someone who's obviously in a position to know, who has no apparent motive to lie.

More often, the agreement is less restrictive. The reporter usually characterizes the source in some way without naming it. That means you want to be sure you know how you'll be described. There are many different ways to refer to a source, and some are more specific than others.

> We can say, "...a government source...",
> "...an administration source...", or
> "...a member of the President's cabinet..."

> We can say, "...a source close to the investigation...", or "...a deputy chief..."

> We can say, "...someone who knew the victim...", or "...a member of the victim's family..."

Obviously, it may make a big difference to you which description we use. In most situations, the reporter will want to be as precise as possible, and you will want it to be as vague as possible. Make sure the two of you agree.

Some sources ask for partial restrictions on the way we identify them. I've done full face interviews with people who ask only that I not give their name, or that I use only their first name. Maybe they don't want their name to leap out of their resume' for the wrong reasons the next time they're looking for a job.

At other times, someone may be willing to give their name, as long as I mask their face. That way they don't have to deal with any confrontations with strangers at the grocery store.

You may also be concerned about other sources the reporter intends to contact. We usually speak with more than one person on a story. That could mean taking the information you've provided and trying to confirm it with someone else, or using it to leverage still more information from them. Do you want that to happen? You may want to ask who else the reporter plans to call, to determine whether it will jeopardize your anonymity.

"On Background"

This is the most ambiguous term used to restrict information, but it's being used more and more widely. Some reporters define it the same way I define "off the record". Others equate it with "not for attribution". In still other instances, some expert or official will speak "on background" to help a reporter reach other sources or find more information relevant to a story. The intent is that the reporter is free to do anything with the information provided–except publish it. For that reason it's sometimes called "not for publication".

With that wide a range of opinion, you want to be very sure your intentions are clear. Or better yet, avoid the term altogether.

"Embargoed"

This is information that can only be used after a certain time, a time that is set out in the embargo. It can be as simple as:

"Embargoed until 9 AM eastern time, Monday, May 1."

Sources use embargoes when they want to allow reporters as much time as possible to prepare the story. The idea is to warn us that the official release is coming, so we can gather all the facts. It also gives the newsmaker time to thoroughly tell those facts, without being rushed by an imminent deadline. Without an embargo, competitive pressures can sometimes lead to a story appearing before we've thoroughly researched it.

Many different organizations use embargoes. The Minnesota Supreme Court releases its decisions to media organizations a day before they are officially issued, and embargoes them until midnight. It's done partly as a courtesy to reporters, so we can begin preparing what are sometimes complex stories ahead of the official announcement. The justices feel their decisions get more accurate and thorough coverage that way.

In this age of satellites, companies sometimes send out embargoed news releases in advance of a news conference that will be beamed nationwide. The printed material provides more detailed information than time permits during the news conference, and sending it ahead allows reporters to formulate questions. It can also serve to increase interest from news organizations. We may not have any reason to cover an announcement by the XYZ Corporation, unless we know what it's going to be about. With an embargo, you can make sure we know what's coming, and still create a media event to trigger the story. It avoids the dilemma of how to notify us of what's coming without undermining the news value of the announcement itself.

The mistake most commonly made with embargoes is to simply announce one, without eliciting any promise from the reporters involved. An embargo is just like any other restriction. It's an agreement between you and the reporter. If I walk into my office and a press release is lying on my desk, it may say "embargoed" on it, but I haven't agreed to anything. Whether I choose to accept that limit, is at my discretion.

Most news organizations routinely honor embargoes out of courtesy, but don't count on it–especially if the story is sensitive. If you expect a reporter to honor your embargo, you'll be wise to ask first. You can do that by making a phone call before you send the release. Or, you can send out a preliminary news release that says certain information is available to anyone who agrees to the embargo. That way a reporter can't get the information without first accepting your terms.

Some negotiation may be appropriate. Perhaps you can allow a reporter to say that an announcement is coming: "Senator Longwind plans to reveal his re-election plans this afternoon." But, the reporter can't disclose what the Senator will say. (Or you simply don't reveal that.) Just be sure you make the same exceptions for everyone.

Some reporters apply the same sort of out clause to embargoes that we use with "off the record" agreements: If we can get the same information somewhere else unembargoed, then we're free to use it.

Embargoes are perhaps the most abused of the agreements I've mentioned. One reason, as I've discussed, is that sources don't always design them properly. However there's a more inherent problem: The penalty for breaking them is often quite mild, compared to the benefits of beating the competition to a story. When was the last time you heard a great public outcry over some reporter breaking an embargo? The source may be upset, and the competing media may be downright ticked. But the offender can always argue that any perceived offense was done in the name of informing the public.

You have more power to enforce an embargo if you're a regular source of information. Reporters think twice about defying the State Supreme Court's embargo, not so much because they're judges, but because they can make us wait for the release of future decisions. Reporters covering the State Capitol usually respect embargoes on budget information or speeches because we want to continue to get that information early.

Be realistic about what you decide to embargo. If it's routine stuff that isn't likely to be anybody's top story of the day, then an informal request for a short delay may be all that's necessary. If you're revealing the name of the ax murderer whose crimes have already been making headlines, don't expect any reporter to patiently wait for your go-ahead. There are times when an embargo simply isn't going to hold, no matter how carefully you design it. Once one news organization breaks an embargo, others will quickly follow. If you don't feel confident that an embargo will be honored, don't create one. Just hold the information until you're ready for it to become public.

"For This Story Only"

That's my term. I know of no standard jargon for this particular restriction, so I invented one. It stems from a problem that's unique to television, and which has a growing number of sources justifiably concerned. The danger is the inappropriate use of file videotape. It's one of the most common mistakes in TV News, and something you need to be aware of, so you can try to protect yourself. It happens more often than we like to admit.

By "file tape" I mean videotape taken for one story, which we then reuse on a different story. News rooms recycle images daily, and it's usually not a problem. But it can be, and if you're the person pictured in an inappropriate way, the result can be embarrassing or worse.

Any decent reporter knows better than to take identifiable pictures of perhaps high school students who are simply going to class, and use them in a story referring to "teenage alcoholics". Such an implication that some innocent students are problem drinkers is grounds for a lawsuit, and may be grounds for the reporter's dismissal.

Unfortunately, what happens is that someone does a story on a topic like underage drinking and simply needs some video to "cover" some of the story's narrative. So the reporter, or some videotape editor, locates some pictures that are already on file and mindlessly inserts them over some controversial reference. In this case the story talks about students, so someone goes and finds some old video of students. The result is that pictures that a reporter wouldn't dream of having a photographer shoot "fresh" for the story, are used because they're conveniently on file. No harm is intended, but the harm done can be serious.

It can happen with all sorts of stories. Perhaps a local battered women's shelter allows a reporter in to do a story. Then it finds the same pictures showing up again and again, every time the topic of battered women is in the news. Video taken of a construction site for a feature story on people who must work on an extremely hot or cold day suddenly appears in another piece on construction accidents. The second story may be one where you would not want to cooperate, if you had the choice, but no one asks.

Most of the time, the use of file tape is harmless. We constantly reuse tape of public figures, just as a newspaper maintains a photo library. We sometimes shoot generic "stock" footage of planes taking off, of the stock exchange or commodity markets, of farms or traffic or local corporate headquarters. It's not possible for me to arrange for someone to videotape the floor of the Legislature every time I need to refer to state lawmakers. So we shoot the House and Senate about once a year and reuse the tape.

Problems arise because file tape is used so routinely by so many people in a news room. We keep every reporter's packaged stories on file after they've been aired. Any other reporter, producer or editor can access them at any time. That includes people who may have had nothing to do with the original story. It's impossible to predict what misjudgments someone might make. The possibilities are infinite. Something as innocent as children on a playground could show up in a story about child abductions. A woman jogging down the street can become "cover video" for a story about rape victims or even prostitution. News rooms are becoming more vigilant about such misuse of video, thanks partly to some expensive lawsuits, and you should be vigilant too.

If the story is controversial, you may want to demand that we use the video only once, and only for the agreed purpose. The more sensitive the topic, the more cautious you should be. If you're being careful about letting a reporter or photographer have access in the first place, then you should be concerned about any future use of that material. When a reporter asks you to cooperate on a story, you may want to say, "I'll do what you want, if..." and make one of the "ifs" an assurance that the video won't be used for any other purpose.

What you're requesting is that the reporter personally make sure that the video is not kept, that any sensitive shots are erased after the story airs. That's really the only way anyone can promise you the video won't somehow be misused in the future. If all you get for assurance is, "Don't worry," worry.

BE PREPARED TO BARGAIN.

The reporter usually expects you to characterize whatever information you want to restrict, before agreeing to restrict it. Just saying, "I want to go off the record," is probably not enough. You're going to have to somehow describe what it is you want to tell us and explain why some restrictions are necessary. You need to explain why the information is relevant to the story, and why it's in the reporter's interest to accept the limits you propose.

In some cases it may be obvious that as an employee, you don't want your boss to know that you're revealing illegal activity by your company or agency. At other times, you may have to explain that you know facts about the subject of a story, which will change what the reporter intends to say, but you want those facts kept secret. Then explain why.

In some situations the reporter will make the first offer. We may ask for information "not for attribution" if it's obvious that's the only way to get it. I've had conversations with sources that go back and forth. It always starts out "on the record" (Great Rule # 1), but if someone is reluctant to answer my questions and I can understand why, I may suggest we go "off the record". Then once I know what the information is, it's sometimes possible to persuade a source to put at least some of it back "on the record," or at least "not for attribution".

I'm using the standard terms here for the sake of convenience, but like many reporters, I'm using them less and less in practice. They're so frequently misunderstood. Instead, I may say something like, "We can protect your identity," and then explain exactly how I propose to do that.

SEEING THE UNSEEABLE

Protecting a source is a little more complicated in television than in print because we usually still need something on videotape. If you're accusing someone of wrongdoing, we prefer to have you make the accusations directly, even if we can't reveal who you are. If you've agreed to relate your experiences about being a victim of rape or abuse, we want to hear your account in your words. So, we arrange the interview so that viewers can't recognize you. We may use a "silhouette" interview in which we light you from behind. Then the camera sees only a black silhouette. We can also shoot a normal interview and later disguise it with electronic techniques that graphically distort the image or alter the pitch of the voice.

Sometimes it's a simple matter of changing the camera angle. A few years ago I did a story about alleged child sex abuse. The chief accuser was the mother, and she allowed us to videotape her two children from behind, as they watched cartoons on TV. I've also done impromptu interviews in sensitive situations where I've had the camera shoot from behind over a person's shoulder. The picture shows me listening, and perhaps the back of the person's head.

All of these techniques are subject to negotiation. Some TV stations now have written agreements that explain what techniques we will use. No reporter can give you an absolute guarantee that no one watching will figure out who you are. The important thing is to be sure you understand what steps we will take to prevent that from happening, and that you're satisfied with that level of protection.

A QUESTION OF AUTHORITY

The use of confidential sources is undergoing an intense review among journalists. One reason is the infamous case of former *Washington Post* reporter, Janet Cooke. After she wrote a Pulitzer Prize winning profile of a child drug-addict, she admitted that the child–whose identity she said she was protecting–didn't exist. The incident was acutely embarrassing to the *Post*. It raised troubling questions for news organizations everywhere. Editors and news directors must ask themselves just how much they can trust individual reporters. No news manager wants to be the next one to be "Cooked."

More recently, the owners of the *Minneapolis Star Tribune* and the *St. Paul Pioneer Press* were sued for revealing a source who had been promised anonymity. The source was a media relations consultant named Dan Cohen. Cohen was a campaign associate of the 1982 Republican candidate for Minnesota governor. Just before the '82 election, Cohen offered reporters information that he said they were free to use or not use. He wouldn't reveal what the information was, but he made them promise not to name him as their source if they used it. Reporters for both papers agreed and Cohen then gave them documents that showed that the Democratic candidate for lieutenant governor had been convicted of shoplifting and charged with unlawful assembly more than a decade earlier. The shoplifting conviction had later been set aside and the other charge had been dismissed.

Editors at each of the newspapers saw it as a political smear tactic. After some heated internal debate, they decided their readers had a right to know who provided the information. So they overruled the reporters and disclosed that Cohen was the source.

In a landmark case, Cohen sued and the court awarded him $700,000 in damages for breach of contract. The Minnesota Supreme Court later reversed the ruling, deciding in favor of the newspapers. Then, on appeal to the U.S. Supreme Court, the Justices ruled that Cohen did have the right to sue, and that the First Amendment did not absolve the newspapers of responsibility for the reporters' promises.

As a result of these and other cases, many news organizations now give reporters less leeway in granting anonymity to a source. Some editors require reporters to check with management before entering into an agreement to protect a source's identity or withhold information. That editor may even want to know who the source is. That means you need to make sure that the reporter you're dealing with has the authority to do what he or she promises. Again, if you're not sure, ask. You also want to find out who else may be given your name, and how far they're willing to go to protect you.

Be careful with a producer or staffer, other than a reporter, who offers you assurances. It's the reporter on the story and the reporter's bosses who are responsible for deciding what to include in a story, not some person who may have talked you into doing an interview. Don't be confused by titles. A producer may be acting at the direction of a reporter or vice versa, but in every case, *You need to reach agreement with whomever receives the information.* Whenever someone makes promises to you, be sure you know exactly who that person is, and be sure the same promises are made by anyone else who will have that information.

DON'T EVER ASSUME YOU'RE PROTECTED.

Don't ever assume that a reporter will withhold information, no matter how sensitive it may be. (Great Rule # 1) There was a time when a reporter wouldn't think of naming the victim of a rape, or identifying a juvenile victim of abuse, but that time is gone. Many news organizations now consider it acceptable to name the accuser in a rape trial. Some women's advocates argue that the only way to remove the stigma of rape is to routinely identify rape victims.

As child abuse has become a major issue, there are great pressures to identify its victims, if not by name, certainly by circumstance. When we name an accused parent, for all practical purposes we've often named the child.

It may seem like an obvious courtesy to withold the address of a crime victim, but many reporters will reveal that. There's usually no malicious intent. It's just that we're accustomed to passing along any relevant facts.

If you have concerns about any information related to a story, say so. Sometimes a polite request is all it takes. If that isn't enough, do whatever bargaining you can. Appeal to the reporter's sense of decency and good will. That may sound naive, but it works more often than you might think.

Even expert media handlers sometimes get burned, because they're lulled into a false sense of security. They find they can sometimes talk casually to reporters without being quoted. Sources who have the power to retaliate against reporters can sometimes become overconfident. A key government figure, a police source or an organization's spokesperson may be able to get away with an ill-advised remark occasionally. The reporter who hears it may decide that repeating it isn't a good enough story to justify losing a future source.

But eventually the offense is big enough to motivate one of us to take that risk. The reporter who then "turns on you" may really be someone who's been protecting you from yourself–and finally decides to stop doing it.

BE CAREFUL OUT THERE.

Again, let me emphasize *there is no universal agreement among reporters as to what any of these restrictions mean.* A print colleague of mine says that he defines "off the record" the way I define "not for attribution", and he believes his sources define it that way. That means if I were a source, I might say something to him that I don't want him to use, and he would think he was free to use it as long as he didn't say who told him. (I would not be happy.) You should always explain exactly what restrictions you want to impose. *Don't use jargon.*

I thought about putting a caution at the beginning of this chapter, something like:

> "Warning: These people are professionals. Don't try this at home!"

Then I realized that many of the people who most need and use these restrictions are people who've never dealt with a reporter. Whistle blowers are usually not veteran media consultants. They're everyday folks, who see a wrong that needs to be exposed. Some of those who have the most justification for staying anonymous are not regular newsmakers. They're innocent crime victims, or people who are powerless to challenge someone in authority.

Successfully negotiating with a reporter requires that you understand what your options are, and what risks you're taking. Speaking off the record or anonymously to a reporter is one of the riskiest things you can do. It can also be one of your most effective tools.

CHAPTER NINE:

SPIN

"Spin" and the professional "spin doctors" who use it, have gotten a rather bad rap from professional journalists. The term has come to have a negative connotation, suggesting that someone is trying to substitute his or her biases for the reporter's "objectivity". In its most cynical form, spin is nothing more than sophistry, an attempt to obscure the facts. But spin can also be positive or simply neutral. As I'm using the term here, it means nothing more than an attempt to influence the way a news story is told. That, as I've already said, is the prerogative of any source.

When a political candidate's lieutenants fan out after a speech to give their "interpretation", or when corporate spokespeople argue on behalf of their bosses, they're not coercing reporters into some predetermined bias. They might like to, but they don't have that power. They're simply making sure that their views are heard and considered. What takes them a step beyond merely voicing an opinion, is that they understand how a reporter is likely to respond and they adjust their message to try to direct that response. Just as a skilled tennis player can put spin on a ball, and completely change its direction and speed, you can often redirect a story with a little skillful "spin".

THE ENGLISH IS ALREADY THERE.

Reporting is not a passive exercise. We're trained to observe but that doesn't mean we simply pass along a collection of facts. Rather, we fit facts into stories, and that requires some interpretation. By the time you receive a call, the reporter has some tentative story in mind. It may be an idea the reporter is checking out before suggesting the story to his editors. Or it may be something already discussed and assigned. A scientist would call it a "hypothesis". It's some idea that we then check against reality.

That may sound a little backwards, but keep in mind that stories don't fall out of the sky. We have to go find them. To do that, we must have at least a vague idea of what we're looking for. As I said in the first chapter, every story must pass the, "So what?" test. If we can't at least imagine a possible answer to that question, it's not a potential story to us.

Some of the stories we cover are driven by events. If that's something unexpected, such as a fire, murder or plane crash, we call it "spot news". (With typical gallows humor, one photographer I know calls it "splat" news.) Other stories are based on planned events such as rallies, demonstrations or news conferences, which we may decide to cover. Still other stories begin as a tip from someone. In many cases they start out as nothing more than speculation by a reporter or assignment editor.

In every case, it's the reporter's job to check on it. If it's a fire, is it a "three alarm with injuries," or just "food on the stove?" If we're speculating that retail sales may be down this Christmas because of the economy, what do retailers think? What are they willing to say about it? The answers to those questions will either confirm the story, change it, or kill it altogether–and that's where you come in.

When you speak to a reporter, you're providing the answers that will determine what the story will or won't be. It's your opportunity to put spin on it (or change the reporter's spin). If the reporter calls and says, "How's business?" and you say, "Fine," you may have just killed an intended story about declining sales. If you say, "Great!" you may be changing it to one about how surprisingly good sales are. Instead of reporting, "Holiday retail sales are off this season, due to a bad economy," the reporter may decide that the opposite is true. We may say, "Despite a weak economy, some local merchants say sales are brisk this Christmas."

Sometimes a reporter is trying to see if you "fit" a planned story. Perhaps we already have the latest retail sales figures–which are down–and we need some illustration. If you say, "Yes, my business is hurting," you may become that illustration. If you say your business is good, we may not use you at all because you don't confirm the numbers. Or we may use you as a counterpoint to show that not all merchants are suffering. With that simple one-sentence answer to a reporter's first question, you may be determining what the story will be about, whether you're part of it, and what your role will be. That's considerable influence.

You're not dictating to the reporter what the story should be; you're simply giving information, and *You should be giving your assessment of that information.* Some of my colleagues differ with me here. They say what a good reporter should be seeking is the objective truth about Christmas sales. The numbers are either up or they're down. "That's a fact," they say, "and that fact is what the story should be based on." It's rarely that simple. Bare facts alone don't make a story. What makes a story is how those facts affect things–including you–and that's more subjective.

The reporter is judging your response according to the planned story, and judging the story according to your response, wondering, "Does this fit?" If not, "How can I make it fit?" The criterion is not just, "Do I have the truth?" It's also, "Do I have a good story?" The secret of the spin doctors is the realization that any fact is subject to interpretation. We not only need to know what's happening; we must somehow analyze that information, if only to decide whether it's a story. Why shouldn't you attempt to influence those decisions?

CHOOSE THE REPORTER

One of the first and most effective ways to influence a story, is often overlooked: Choose who tells it. In many situations, *You can pick the reporter.* The most obvious way is to call one, as Brian Coyle did. (chapter 4) But you may still have that choice, when we call you. Your availability is a commodity. You can give it to that reporter, you can withhold it, or you can give it to someone else. It's an option you have with each piece of information you possess, or access that you can offer. You can reward a favored reporter with more, and penalize a distrusted one by giving less.

It's not unusual for newsmakers to be selective about who they talk to. When Ross Perot was running for president, I was assigned to do a profile on him. So, I made a call to his campaign and requested an interview. His staff politely informed me that they would add me to the list–a list they said numbered about 3-thousand! I didn't get an interview, but you can bet that my bosses and I would have been thrilled if I had. Larry King and Barbara Walters had much better success, and nobody pulled their names out of a hat.

Few of us will ever be in as much demand as Mr. Perot, but who you are isn't as critical as the story you can tell. When you make news, you have something a reporter or perhaps all reporters want. The bigger the story, the more valuable you are. Whether you're a witness to a crime or a congressional candidate, you're probably someone we'd like to interview. That's leverage you can use.

Choose the Medium.

Do you want the brief treatment and broad reach of television news? Would you prefer that a longer more detailed version appear first in the newspaper? Do you want a still longer version in a weekly or monthly magazine? Television is the quickest way to get the word out, if your concern is damage control. On the other hand, there's usually less time to thoroughly explain yourself. The medium where the story will appear is the first criterion you should use when deciding who to talk to (chapter 6).

Would you rather have a reporter package your story, or would you prefer to appear on a talk show and tell it yourself? Is it important that you reach the mass audience that watches news in the evening, or the older and largely female audience that watches daytime news and talk shows?

What you should do depends on the story and the circumstances. Sometimes the appropriate choice is, "All of the above."

Choose the Outlet.

One of the adages of selling media advertising is that business owners tend to place ads on the station they watch or listen to personally, or in the newspaper they read. The same is true for people with news tips. Whether you're responding to a request from a reporter or seeking one out, it makes sense to deal with an organization that you like. If you prefer the way some newspaper or station handles other stories, you're more likely to be pleased with the way it tells your story.

News organizations develop reputations over time, and there are usually good reasons for those reputations. Your story will get a very different treatment in the *New York Times* than it will in the *National Enquirer*. It will look different on the *CBS Evening News*, from the way it will look on *Geraldo* or *Hard Copy*.

Choose the Person.

Unless you're a frequent newsmaker or a news junkie, the odds are you won't know the reporter who calls you. Even in television, reporters rarely become household names. (Anchors do, but not reporters.) That puts you at an immediate disadvantage. If you're someone who has reason to be in the news from time to time, I strongly suggest you get to know the reporters in your community.

No, I don't mean call and ask them out to lunch. Watch their work. Get a feel for how they treat stories, particularly stories related to your field or business. Are they fair? Are their stories accurate?

Regular newsmakers tend to develop relationships with the reporters who cover a specific beat. Such sources may have a track record with reporters and vice versa. If you've dealt with a reporter before, you may already know whether you're at risk of being quoted out of context, or whether you can speak safely "off the record".

Sometimes a reporter develops a specialized style, as perhaps an investigative reporter or consumer advocate. If you get a call at your business from a guy who handles a different consumer complaint each night on TV, you don't need a Ph.D. to figure out why he's calling you. Investigative reporters are usually looking for some wrong to expose, some villain to reveal. You need to find out if that supposed villain is you. The more you can learn about the reporters in your community before one calls, the better equipped you'll be to make some informed decisions when that happens.

Choose an Expert.

Obviously, you want to try to deal with someone who understands what you're saying. Sometimes that's a specialist or "beat reporter", someone who's already dealt with the topic. Like most news rooms, mine has a full-time medical reporter, but it's become a job that one person can't always handle. The public's appetite for medical and health news has grown dramatically in recent years. At times, she's already on assignment when some health related story breaks. I've filled in on medical stories occasionally, and it's not unusual for a doctor or researcher to greet me with some skepticism. "Why isn't

Susan covering this?" is a fair question from a doctor. He's dealt with her, but he's never seen me before.

I was once sent to cover a new research finding on AIDS. It was when the AIDS epidemic was making headlines almost daily, and public fears and confusion about the disease were rampant. I met with a researcher in his lab and before he would begin the interview, he grilled me on my understanding of the disease. He asked questions like, "Do you understand exactly what it means for a person to be HIV positive?" I did, but he was wise to ask.

The doctor could simply have refused to do the interview. He or the medical center's public relations folks could have demanded that a more knowledgeable reporter be assigned to the story if he felt I wasn't qualified. I know he would have preferred to see the story killed, rather than have his research misinterpreted. He did agree to talk to me. I'm sure it helped that I was willing to listen to his concerns.

When you're calling a reporter to suggest a story, call a political reporter about politics, a business reporter about business and so forth. If you don't know who that is, just call your preferred news organization and someone will be happy to tell you who covers that beat.

Choose Your Bias.

I know it's fashionable to talk about "media bias". But when it comes to dealing with reporters, it's an assumption that works about as well as cutting meat with a baseball bat. The result is messy at best, and you have rather limited chances of success. The fact is most news rooms are quite diverse. Not only do you find racial, ethnic and gender diversity; you also find a wide diversity of opinions. News rooms are full of Republicans,

Democrats and Independents; Liberals and Conservatives; folks who are Pro- and Anti-Abortion Rights; whatever.

In other words: yes, we have biases. We're human. However those biases are individual, not collective–and that's to your advantage. Some reporters are more sympathetic to certain viewpoints than others, and it's sometimes possible to determine who's who. You do it the same way you decide what news to watch or what magazines you read. You look at our work, at how we handle stories. What you should be looking for is not a reporter who sounds like an advocate for your cause. That's not our job. Look for someone who you feel will treat you fairly. That may turn out to be someone who personally disagrees with you, but who shows sympathy and respect for you and your opinions.

Where personal biases show up most often is not in the telling of a story. That's where we're most conscious of the need to be balanced and fair. Instead, our biases tend to surface when we select stories. That process is much more subjective. A reporter who has children is more likely to share concerns about funding for education. One who has a phobia about AIDS is not going to ask to do a story about hospice care for its victims. The presence of women in news rooms that were once almost totally male, has led to increased coverage of issues affecting women.

You can use those biases to your advantage. If you want to talk about school finances, call a parent; when the topic is access for the handicapped, call someone who has shown sensitivity to that issue in the past.

A word of caution: Don't ask us how we feel about some controversy. Most of us will politely decline to answer. When we do answer, the response is more likely to be one calculated to win your confidence than a true statement about how we feel. We know why you're asking.

A bigger word of caution: Don't tell a reporter, "I want you to do this story because you agree with me." First, it's a tremendous professional insult. We consider it our job to make a distinction between our personal opinions and the objectivity that we strive for when we cover a story. Worse, the effect could be the opposite of what you want. Reporters who think they're perceived as biased, often go out of their way to prove that accusation wrong. That tendency could result in a less favorable story. If you feel you must play upon a reporter's motives, say something like, "I trust you to be fair."

Choose Experience.

Given a choice between a novice reporter and one with experience, choose experience. It may be tempting to think that an inexperienced reporter might be more malleable, easier to sway to your way of thinking. Often the opposite is true. Changing a story typically requires some improvisation. A different story may mean that we need different interviews, different questions, different video. The ability to do that and still make deadline is something we learn over time. As we do our jobs, we get better at reinventing stories when it's necessary. Reporters with less experience are often less flexible simply because they don't know how to make the necessary changes.

Another problem is that an editor generally gives less experienced reporters less latitude. They're more likely to be working on stories that were assigned to them rather than ones they pitched themselves. An editor who is willing to defer to the judgment of an experienced reporter in the field is often less willing to trust a newcomer. A veteran reporter may even have the clout to kill a story if you make a convincing case that the facts don't support it. A rookie may be under greater pressure to "make it work."

We Don't All Play by the Same Rules.

Reporters are perhaps the ultimate practitioners of situation ethics. We tend to subscribe to the principle espoused by the Navy's first female Admiral, Rear Admiral Grace Hopper. When asked how she managed to get so far in such a male-dominated bureaucracy, she answered that she'd learned, "It's easier to ask forgiveness, than it is to get permission." To a reporter, that sometimes translates, "Get the story, and worry about explaining yourself later." If that involves misleading someone about our intentions or failing to check out certain facts, there are plenty of plausible denials that the reporter can make later: "That isn't what I said. You must have misunderstood," or, "Our competitor had the story too, so we had to rush it." Unlike the admiral, we probably won't even ask for your forgiveness.

Few reporters will admit to deliberately lying to get a story, but we all know of instances when one of us has. Some (including myself) will say they can conceive of circumstances in which they would condone it. We're not above giving you just enough information to allow you to draw incorrect conclusions about what our intentions are. If some new information leads us to change out intentions, we don't always feel obligated to disclose that.

Some journalists and scholars argue that our principles *should* vary. They say for freedom of the press to be effective, each reporter has the right and the responsibility to set personal standards. It's not that we have no ethics, it's just that there's no one standard we follow. Those ethical guidelines that do exist–and there are many from such organizations as the Society of Professional Journalists–are vague. They serve as general guidelines for reporters and news rooms, not as a way to predict what a reporter will do. If you're looking for answers to questions like, "When is it permissible to deceive a source?" you won't find much. If you're seeking precise definitions for terms such as "Fairness" and "Accuracy", you'll find no definitive answers.

The guidelines that do exist, are considered advisory. News rooms typically do not subscribe to a specific set of ethical standards. We say that's because we don't want to infringe on a reporter's prerogatives, but there's another concern: Managers fear if they set strict standards, someone could use those standards against us in a lawsuit.

Some of us are more trustworthy than others. You should be more cautious with an unfamiliar reporter (or one that's already burned you) than with one you've dealt with successfully before. The more sensitive the story, the more cautious you should be.

When the Reporter Changes

On an ongoing story, the reporters may change over time. Someone scheduled to work day side will eventually go home, and a night side reporter will take over. At other times, a new development may come up when the original reporter is on another assignment or has the day off.

Let new reporters know that you're glad to help them get up to speed on what's been happening. Yes, you may have to repeat things you've already said and that may seem tedious. Ask yourself, "Who's going to be hurt most if your treatment takes a sudden negative turn? Who has the most to gain if it improves?"

The reporter frequently determines what tack to take on a story, not the news room. If you're unhappy with the coverage you've been getting, you have an opportunity to change it. If you like the way you've been treated, don't assume it will continue. Reinforce it.

There are times when a news room will deliberately change reporters, in an attempt to improve relations with a source. If a reporter's story has offended you, we may send in a fresh face in hopes of again winning your cooperation. Perhaps a reporter has exposed corruption in a local police department. His news room may still need information about other crime stories. Or it may be important to follow up on the scandal by talking to the guilty parties. Sometimes a new reporter is more likely to be successful than the one who broke the story.

When you suspect that kind of tactic is being used against you, it's tempting to stonewall the whole organization, and not "let them off" so easily. Think again. If a news room finds it necessary to change reporters to please you, then it's responding to pressure from *you*. You are "picking" a new reporter, and if that results in more favorable coverage, who wins? If you called an editor and said, "I'm not going to deal with so-and-so anymore; send someone else," you might not get very far. We're understandably defensive about taking orders from sources. So simply make your displeasure obvious, and let us figure it out. You may get a new reporter, and we'll think it was our idea.

Get a Reference.

Sometimes, its important to know who you're dealing with before you talk. Maybe you want to talk "off the record" or "not for attribution" with a new reporter you're not sure you can trust. One way to check them out is with another reporter. We usually have a feel for who can be trusted and who can't, among our colleagues and competitors. Call a reporter you already know and ask, "Is this someone who won't burn me."

If you call someone in the same news organization, the call is likely to have two effects. First, it will get you some sort of feel for the newcomer. The other thing your call may do is get the two reporters talking, about you. You're in effect making your relationship with the second reporter an extension of your relationship with the first. Your friend may say to his colleague, "I have a good relationship with so-and-so and I want to keep it. I've told him you can be trusted, so don't prove me wrong."

When the Reporter's Unprepared

Sometimes it pays to see an uninformed reporter as a blank slate on which you can select the message you want to write. Reporters who haven't done their homework can be the easiest to influence. I once addressed a group of county officials from around the country on the topic of press relations. Some of them were grumbling about the reporter who comes in at the very end of a board meeting and asks one of them, "What happened?"

"Why weren't you here to find out for yourself?" may seem to be the most apt response, but it won't endear you to the reporter. I know it's tempting, but try to resist. As I told those officials, a reporter like that can be a newsmaker's dream. It's like getting a blank check. Take it and run! You're being given an opportunity to characterize events in whatever way you choose. Start spinning.

The Exclusive

This is the ultimate way to pick a reporter. It's a restriction you agree to place on yourself, a promise that you won't cooperate with any other reporter on the same story. Reporters love getting exclusives, and our bosses love us when we get them.

A promise to give a reporter an exclusive can be a powerful tool, a bargaining chip traded for other concessions from the reporter. It's a way for you to maintain some degree of control over the story. Sometimes public figures who face damaging accusations will offer an exclusive interview to a reporter who they believe will go easy on them.

An exclusive arrangement works best when no one else knows about the story. It's a little riskier when more than one reporter is seeking an interview, and it means turning some of them away. Reporters quickly take offense if we feel a competitor is getting favored treatment. A perceived slight could result in less favorable coverage from some other reporter.

It's a good idea to keep the relationships positive whenever possible. Ideally, you want to maneuver yourself into a situation where you can say to a reporter, "Yes, I will talk to you," rather than, "No, I won't talk." Your best strategy may be to go ahead and cooperate with an unsympathetic reporter—and then go find a sympathetic one.

CHOOSE YOUR ADVERSARIES

When you're uncomfortable with a reporter's approach to a story, you may be better off trying to change the approach rather than refusing to talk. You can then use your willingness to participate to bargain over how we tell the story. Occasionally, you can even influence who among your critics we use in a story, or at least how we use them.

When my station decided to do an hour-long program on a controversial plan to store spent fuel rods outside a nuclear power plant, we decided to arrange a debate among the opposing interests. There were people on many sides of the issue who wanted to speak. Several environmental groups opposed the project. So did the Indian tribe whose reservation was next to the proposed site. Other nearby residents were divided over the plan, and state and federal officials also had some concerns. The utility, Northern States Power (NSP), feared that so many opposing groups might overwhelm it, if each had its own representative.

NSP demanded to know who they would be facing, and the producer did some negotiating with the company over the format. We considered the desires of the other groups too, but NSP was in a unique position. We knew going into the project that some views would be represented during the "set up" portion of the program rather than as active participants. We felt we could leave some of the other interest groups out of the debate without compromising the integrity of the show. But we could hardly consider the debate complete without the utility's participation.

There was some discussion. We made some adjustments that we considered journalistically fair and acceptable. NSP didn't get everything it had at first demanded, but it did exert some influence. The utility's spokespeople knew they couldn't dictate to us how to do the show, but they had some cards to play and they played them.

You usually have options other than just saying, "Yes," or, "No," to a reporter. If a situation makes you uncomfortable, look for ways to make it acceptable. It was in NSP's interest to participate, to defend its plan. The utility just wanted to be on what it considered a level playing field. Before you decide to refuse a reporter's request, consider whether you want to make a counterproposal. We just might accept it.

CRAFT THE IMAGES.

The power of pictures has long been used to shape the message. Protestors were burning effigies for hundreds of years before there was television. Control the images, and you often control the story. Images can completely alter the impact of a story. They can reinforce or contradict the story's other content, sometimes inadvertently. Some modern communications theories hold that the images, not the content, determine the true message received by a viewer. What people *see* often has greater emotional impact than what a reporter *says*.

It's a phenomenon Hollywood uses very effectively. Special effects can completely alter a viewer's sense of reality. They can convince us that extra terrestrials truly exist (and look like lovable stuffed toys). They can make us believe it's possible to travel through time or inside a human body.

Remember *The Exorcist*, the movie in which a little girl was supposedly possessed by demons? The scenes showing her suffering all sorts of bizarre symptoms of possession were incredibly graphic. (Stuff like her head spinning completely around.) Then to solidify the audience's belief in what was happening, she was taken to see a doctor—who played the classic skeptic. He offered what most of us would consider perfectly rational explanations for what she was going through. How did audiences react? With hoots and howls at the doctor!

In our normal lives, most of us would react to reports of demonic possession just as that doctor did, with some reasoned explanation. A movie creates another reality for us. We were unconsciously saying to ourselves, "I *saw* what happened to her." Our skepticism probably returns once we walk out of the theater, but when we see images in the news, there's no theater to leave.

Sometimes the effect of images is inadvertent. One example that's been circulating since the 1984 presidential race, is about a story done by CBS correspondent Leslie Stahl. The premise of her piece was how effectively President Reagan handled television, and how he used it to camouflage unpopular policies. Her hard-hitting narrative highlighted cuts in funding for such things as education and the disabled, under his administration. To illustrate her points she used video of the President interacting with school children, attending the Special Olympics and among waving flags.

The story was–she thought–so hard hitting that she feared the administration might refuse to cooperate with her afterwards. But the intended irony was apparently lost on the White House. After the story aired, an administration staffer called to *thank* her for the piece, gushing over how wonderful it was. Mystified, she asked what they liked about it. He told her it was all those wonderful images of Reagan showing how much he cared.

Reagan was so good at shedding blame for any problems, that he became know as the "teflon president". His chief image man, Michael Deaver says the White House used images to convey a visceral message about the President. The strategy was to reach voters on an emotional level. The hidden message in images like those

Leslie Stahl used, was that Reagan was in control, and that he really wanted to do the right thing. Deaver argues that if a president can convince the electorate that he means well, they'll tend to ignore his specific policies.

Modern political campaigns revolve around the creation of images designed to put candidates in a favorable light. Sometimes it works. Sometimes it fails. During the 1988 presidential race, the Dukakis campaign wanted to portray its candidate as someone who could be tough militarily. So a photo opportunity was arranged for the press, with the candidate perched on top of a tank wearing combat headgear. It succeeded in creating the desired news coverage, but the image wasn't perceived as intended. To many who saw it, Dukakis came across not as a figure of military authority, but rather silly-looking and out of place.

The opposition loved it. The Republicans took that image and placed it in a Bush campaign ad, with a caption reading, "America can't afford the risk." A Democratic campaign strategist later told me how extremely damaging that mistake was. So much so that some Dukakis operatives thought that one image may have cost him the election.

Sometimes the goal is to hide an image. When a plane crashes, airlines frequently try to cover up their logo on the plane, so when the cameras shoot the crash scene, the airline's name or symbol won't appear. It's not that anyone expects to keep secret whose plane went down. What they want to hide is the image of their name on the wreckage. They know that long after a particular crash has faded into the flying public's memory, the image of a burning plane can remain all too vivid. Airlines want their logo to be a symbol of comfort and safety, untainted by past tragedies.

Often there simply is no story, until there are pictures. In the late '80s, the major television news organizations were criticized for not responding more quickly to the famine in Africa. One reason for the delay was the difficulty of getting reporters into and videotape out of the affected region. Once pictures did get out, they riveted the world's attention for months and prompted massive relief efforts. (Remember *We Are the World*?) There had been earlier reports in print, and while those stories were troubling, they did not result in the action that the video images prompted.

Again in 1992, images led to direct U.S. military intervention to protect famine relief efforts in Somalia. When camera crews greeted the marines as they landed on the beach, it seemed awkward to some. As *Time* magazine noted, "...wasn't it also appropriate? In a sense it was cameras that had sent them there."

At the very least, the ability to get pictures will change the threshold for whether television considers a story viable. The harder it is to get pictures, the stronger the other merits of the story must be. Exceptionally good pictures will make up for a multitude of other weaknesses.

Creativity Counts.

A single creative image can take a ho-hum story and make it compelling, even if it's an event contrived solely for the cameras. It worked for U.S. Senator Paul Wellstone, who took office just as the Persian Gulf War was about to begin. He won an upset election victory with a campaign that was heavy on imagery, and he went to Washington as Congress' most vocal opponent of a U.S. invasion of Kuwait. Soon after he arrived in Washington, his staff staged a media event that was as effective as it was elegantly simple.

As Senator-elect, Wellstone had held a series of town meetings. It was a time when U.S. troops were heading to the Middle East, so the imminent threat of war was a frequent topic at those meetings. What Wellstone heard was fear about the prospect of sending sons and daughters into combat.

By the time he got to Washington, his anti-war views were well known. He would later take a leading role in the Congressional debate over whether to send in the troops. In the meantime, how does a rookie senator make news out of something everybody already knows? How does a novice Democrat pressure a Republican president? A clever former reporter working with Wellstone's staff knew exactly how.

Wellstone was scheduled to meet with Vice President Dan Quayle as part of a reception for new members of Congress. It was the kind of gathering that deserves at most a brief mention in the news back home. This time it would become lead story material. The Senator's staff had a tape recording of his town meetings. So they decided to "give it" to Quayle.

A sizable contingent of reporters had followed Wellstone to Washington and the Senator-elect's staff notified them that they should be sure to cover the reception. Then, when it was Wellstone's turn to shake the Vice President's hand, the Senator graciously handed him the tape. He explained what it contained. He asked Quayle to listen to it, and asked him to forward it to the President, all on camera. It was a flagrant breach of Washington protocol, which alone made it newsworthy. Quayle, of course, accepted the tape and promised to give it to President Bush. What else could he do? The incident immediately became part of Washington legend, and was featured prominently on everyone's evening news back home.

If you can find ways to enhance the pictures, you increase the likelihood that we will tell the story. If you want to draw attention to the plight of the homeless, show someone who's homeless and how they live. If you want to talk about drunk drivers, show an accident caused by a drunk. A few years ago, the crumpled wreckage of a car from a multi-fatal accident was hoisted onto a billboard over a Twin Cities freeway. A single sentence above it read: "Sometimes it takes a family of four to stop a drunk driver." It not only caught the attention of thousands of motorists; the billboard, and the story behind it, made national news.

When We Need Your Help

In some situations, the reporter is forced to rely on you to find illustrations. When an Attorney General's office or Better Business Bureau exposes some consumer scam, one of the first things a reporter will ask is, "Can you give me the name of a victim?" At other times, a reporter may decide to do a story on some public issue and need to personalize it. Who do we call? Usually some interest group. If the topic is business taxes, we need a business owner who's affected. So we may ask a business lobbyist to suggest someone. If the topic is child abuse, we may look for an abused child by calling one of the many children's advocacy organizations; or we may seek out an offender by contacting a treatment center. We are in constant need of illustrations and that's typically how we find them.

We don't like to admit it, but when we turn to such groups, we are in effect granting them a degree of control over our stories. If you're picking who the reporter talks to, you have some control over what's said and therefore what direction the story may take. Less is left to chance.

You're not counting on the reporter to find someone who happens to be a good illustration of your view, instead of someone who may contradict you. A competent reporter will maintain a healthy skepticism of any situation that someone else has orchestrated. But if there's a good story in it, we'll follow your lead.

Reporters are under constant pressure to dramatize stories. Help us do that and you'll increase the likelihood that we'll tell it your way. Leave the drama to us, and you risk having a reporter take the story somewhere you don't want it to go.

When we ask for your help, take it as an opportunity to spin.

Look the Part.

Another thing to keep in mind is your personal image. You may be speaking the great truths of the universe, but if you look uncertain or defensive, you risk losing considerable credibility. Viewers tend to be fairly sophisticated in judging what they see. They understand that a crime victim may be upset, or that a homemaker may look nervous simply because she's not accustomed to being on camera. They're not as understanding when an executive is unable or unwilling to defend the actions of her company, or when a government official waffles on questions about alleged abuse of power. If you're not used to being on camera, at least make sure you're comfortable with what you have to say.

The best images reinforce the message you want to send. When a group of corporate raiders led by Al Checchi bought Northwest Airlines, they called a news conference to announce their intentions. The last thing they wanted to look like was a bunch of overpaid financiers waiting for the profits to roll in. The message they wanted to send was, "We're going to get to work and make this a great airline." It was a message intended not only for the public, but for their employees–the people whose confidence they needed most. Checchi and other top executives walked into the news conference and casually took off their suit coats–on camera.

A friend of mine who was covering it, turned to Northwest's head of corporate communications and asked admiringly, "Was this your idea?" His answer was a big smile.

HELP. DON'T HINDER.

A photographer I frequently work with has a running gag. Whenever I can't get someone to talk to me or allow me some sort of access, Aethan pretends to be speaking to the person. With mock drama he asks, *"What are you trying to hide?!"* We both smile, but we're only half joking. As I've said before, the reporter's primary goal is to get a story. Whoever helps with that goal is a friend. Anyone who tries to obstruct us is an enemy. The point is simple: If someone is going to be writing or saying things about you for all the world to hear, how do you want that person to perceive you? Above all else, *A reporter is going to judge you according to whether you're cooperative.*

Be Accessible.

As Business Editor, I once had occasion to contact Minneapolis financier Irwin Jacobs. It was in the mid-80s, when corporate raiders were making headlines almost daily, and Jacobs was one of them. He had already amassed a considerable fortune buying up companies, and he was rumored to be on the prowl for more. I dialed his office and when a voice answered, "Irwin Jacobs," I was so surprised I didn't know what to say at first. As any reporter will tell you, business executives are notoriously hard to reach. I expected to go through at least an administrative assistant or two, if not wait hours for him to get out of meetings and return my call. Here was a man who surely thought he had better things to do than take questions from some reporter he'd never met. Yet he answered his own phone, and was perfectly willing to talk.

It wasn't some fluke on the secretary's day off. I soon found that almost whenever I called, he picked up his phone and talked, and not just to me. A year or two later, I was doing a profile piece on him. After doing an interview on location, we returned to his office to tape him working. As he walked in, his assistant handed him a stack of phone messages. While we videotaped, he began returning the calls. One of them was from a reporter from the *Wall Street Journal*. As I stood and listened, Jacobs fielded questions about more takeover rumors. By this time I'd dealt with him on a number of occasions, and his openness still amazed me. The takeover game is one of very high stakes brinkmanship. It's an atmosphere where an ill-advised public statement can undo a deal worth millions, or violate securities laws.

Jacobs wasn't some novice playing catch with financial hand grenades. He knew exactly what he was doing. He recognized that he was operating in a very public arena, an arena where the messengers often play a crucial role. He knows the rules, what he can and *can't* say (Great Rule #3). He chooses his words carefully–but he talks.

I'm sure he also realizes that by keeping communication open, he's gaining information as well as giving it. (Just what are the latest rumors about that deal?) He's also building a reputation as a source who cooperates, developing relationships with reporters all across the country, learning how they operate, and perhaps which ones to trust. He's also able to quickly provide input–in other words, to spin.

Jacobs isn't some media hound. He doesn't run around calling news conferences. He doesn't need to. Sometimes just answering the phone is much more effective.

The Control Thing.

At the opposite end of the spectrum from Irwin Jacobs are those who go out of their way to be obstructive. I'm convinced that some people delight in dominating reporters. They typically come from the ranks of people who like being in control: cops, judges, business executives. They're the same people who avoid the media entirely when they can. They're often experienced professionals who should know how to handle such situations. But, to borrow a cliché: They just don't get it.

Take the case of a police chief I once encountered. When an estranged husband held his wife hostage at gun point, news crews descended on the chief's community. We headed straight to the scene. The police officers there were friendly, but they told us they were under strict orders not to talk to us. To get information, we would have to go to City Hall, a couple of miles away.

I needed to know what was happening, but I wasn't about to take my photographer to another location for an interview. I didn't dare. We had no way of knowing at what moment the man might give himself up, or run out guns blaring, or when police might decide to suddenly go in after him. No appeal to reason could persuade any spokesperson to come to the scene–where the story was happening–to brief us. No officer could get permission to provide even the barest details.

I finally made a trip to City Hall without a camera, to get a few basic questions answered, but it was too far to keep going back and forth. Several of us were doing live reports. So, to stay on top of developments, we had to gently "milk" information from some of the authorities who had come from other jurisdictions to help (and who sympathized with our plight). That meant instead of getting the facts from those in charge, we had to rely on people who had second-hand information at best. That's not the ideal way to gather news. It's certainly not the best way for any organization to disseminate it to us. Were we accurate? I think so, but no thanks to the people who should have been most concerned about our accuracy.

All of this might quickly have been forgotten, excused as the result of pressure in a tense situation. But the cooperation didn't improve when the crisis ended. Hours later, police finally coaxed the man into releasing his wife and surrendering. Good police work had triumphed. It was time for a public servant to note his accomplishment, right? The police chief apparently didn't quite see it that way. He called us to a news conference at City Hall, but gave only a minimal account of what happened, and refused to discuss anything more.

Question after question went unanswered. When he didn't want to release the name of the victim, that was perhaps understandable. But he refused to give even the most mundane details. Who had negotiated the release? How many people were on the team that had communicated with the man by phone? Questions that reporters ask routinely following a crime, he ignored or gave only a limited response. Had this couple had problems before? Did this man have a prior criminal record? For what?

Finally, in exasperation I asked, "Why is it necessary to keep so many things about this case secret?"

A smug, "Because I don't want to tell you," was his response, not even pretending that it was necessary.

The chief said, "I won't answer that," so many different ways and so many times, that I was tempted to string all of his answers together into one long series of soundbites. Then preface it with, "This is how willing police are to talk about the case." (I didn't.)

The chief did nothing illegal. Nowhere is it written that he had to provide a spokesperson at the scene. Investigators often withhold certain information. But what was the point? The crime was over and the suspect was in custody.

If the chief's goal was to make "those reporters" jump through his hoops, he succeeded. If he wanted to make me angry, he was very successful. I wanted to strangle the guy! The favorable coverage–which I did give him–came in spite of his attitude. I didn't make him look like the jerk I thought he was, although I gave it some thought.

Maybe he wasn't acting simply out of arrogance. Perhaps it was a crude attempt at media management. The mistake he made was confusing "controlling the message" with "controlling the messengers". When you start ordering reporters around, when you refuse to answer reasonable questions, you're not increasing the likelihood that we'll do and say what you want. You're decreasing it.

Unfortunately such attitudes are common. Some of my colleagues are no doubt chuckling a little at how mild this chief's offenses were. Most police departments restrict what officers can say to a reporter. But the enlightened ones at least provide an alternative spokesperson, someone whose job it is to cooperate rather than obstruct.

No doubt many people hold reporters in contempt. (Maybe you've been cheering for the chief.) But there's a simple choice to make. If you want to alienate the press, start arbitrarily ordering us around; ignore our deadlines;

make sure we suit only your convenience; withhold important information. If instead, you want to build a cooperative relationship, cooperate.

Nice Touches

Thankfully, the scorn for the media that characterizes some organizations is balanced by the actions of others. The chief of the police department in Bloomington, Minnesota recently sent written commendations to each of the reporters and photographers who covered a murder there. He had used the media to appeal for help from the public, and it worked. Someone who saw our reports, tipped police about a suspect and they made an arrest. The commendations were the chief's way of saying, "Thanks." Now *that's* unusual.

There are those who go out of their way to accommodate the press; the hospital that sets aside parking spaces in a crowded lot when they hold a news conference; the corporate spokesperson who offers to carry a photographer's tripod. Such gestures don't guarantee favorable coverage and aren't always deserved. But they are a way to win friends and influence the press corps.

MAKING YOUR APPEAL

Ultimately, putting spin on a story comes down to salesmanship. As sales trainers sometimes put it, speak about "benefits", not "features". In other words, don't just describe what you have. Don't just spout facts. Tell us why we should care. Tell us what's so great about your approach. Appeal to the reporter's compassion, sense of fairness or news judgment. Don't underestimate the value of appeals to ethical or journalistic standards. Asking most reporters to be fair, is like asking a mother to love her child. We think it's something we're already doing. A convincing argument that we're not being fair will at least make most reporters pause and think.

Too many media relations people tend to think of the reporter as someone they must somehow get around. They see us as an obstacle and their strategy is to try to get past us. A more realistic approach is to see the reporter as the first person you must convince. Maybe instead of being a barrier between you and the public, we're a kind of litmus test of the public's reaction. That's certainly what we're trying to be. If a room full of reporters is skeptical of what you say, maybe you need to rethink the message. We're not so very different from everyone else.

To change a story, you can't just criticize it. Sometimes you have to offer a positive alternative. Try to imagine another story that you can suggest, using the same facts, or by adding a few new ones. Maybe your version of what happened is something more than just your response. Maybe it calls into question the reporter's whole approach to the story.

The same situation may be a story about police breaking up a violent demonstration, or about police brutality. It's often in the eye of the beholder. Is an employee the victim of illegal discrimination, or is the company a victim of outrageous accusations from a former disgruntled worker? Make your case.

RESPOND QUICKLY.

Allow time for the reporter to adjust. A story that's sketched in pencil at 8 AM, may have a whole newscast built around it by 4 in the afternoon. Don't wait until the last minute to make your appeal. The later it gets, the fewer options the reporter has. The closer it gets to deadline, the tougher it is for the reporter to make changes and the more some producer or editor may be counting on the story that was assigned. If your contact with the reporter begins with a phone call, that's when you should start spinning, not hours later when you schedule the interview. If there's data you need to collect, do it ASAP and fax it to us. Don't overwhelm us with a hundred page report an hour before deadline.

The need for a quick response is another reason to be available and cooperative whenever possible. The sooner you respond to a reporter's call, the sooner you know what spin you may need to put on the story, and the more time you have to do it. I'm sure it seems like an imposition to jump whenever a reporter calls, but don't be too hard on us. There isn't a reporter alive who wouldn't like more time to do stories. We don't usually have the luxury of picking our deadlines.

LET US KNOW WHAT YOU THINK.

Once a story has appeared, it's too late to change it, but it's not too late to talk about it. Call or write to the reporter and offer your thoughts, favorable or unfavorable. If you don't like something, you can at least plant an idea that might get you more favorable coverage in the future. If you do like something, positive comments never hurt.

Always strive to leave the impression that you're someone who watches, reads, or listens to our stories. When you grant an interview, be sure to ask when the story will appear. Request a copy of it. We'll probably tell you to record it on your VCR, but there's another reason for asking. It sends a subtle reminder that you're part of the reporter's audience. It reinforces in the reporter's mind that you care what the story is and that you'll be paying attention.

Don't be like the guy who came up to me as I was trying to catch a presidential candidate one night. He stopped me in the hall and barked,

"When are you guys going to start covering the issues instead of all this other bull_ _ _ _?"

I said, "As a matter of fact, the story I just aired on the 5 o'clock news tonight was about the issues. Did you see it?"

"Who are you with?" he asked as he looked at the logo on the side of the camera. "Oh, I never watch *your* news."

CHAPTER TEN:

DAMAGE CONTROL

When I was much younger and braver than I am now, I took a weekend course in skydiving with some friends of mine. (Bungee jumping wasn't invented yet.) Before they allowed us to jump, even with a parachute that deployed automatically, we spent several hours in ground school. We learned the proper position and technique for throwing ourselves to the tender mercies of so much sailcloth and cording. We also learned what to do when something goes wrong. I hadn't realized that there are predictable ways for a parachute to fail–and ways to save yourself when that happens. They told us what to do if we had a "Mae West", so named (before the days of political correctness) because it's when one of the cords is caught over the top of the chute, leaving it in the shape of a giant bra. Another possible malfunction, we learned, was the "streamer". I'm sure you get the picture.

We might have been tempted to ignore some of the many precautions they taught us. We knew that with the few jumps we expected to make, the odds were against us having any trouble. But the stakes were too high. Any trouble is major when you're falling from several thousand feet. I distinctly remember our instructor telling us to, "Assume you're going to have a malfunction. It may be on your hundredth jump, or it may be your first," he asserted, "but it's going to happen."

The same holds true for dealing with reporters. Assume you're going to have a malfunction. It may be your first encounter or your fiftieth, but it's coming. Sometimes it's deliberate and sometimes it's inadvertent, but it happens. (I realize I'm not building your confidence here.) The good news is, just like parachuting, the malfunctions come in predictable ways. You can prepare yourself. You can learn how to do "damage control".

BEFORE YOU GET BURNED

What that skydiving instructor taught us wasn't how to pick up the pieces after we hit the ground. That's usually too late. Whenever possible, you want to prevent damage from happening. Harm done to your business or reputation is not easy to correct after a story has aired or appeared in print. Even if you succeed in getting a retraction or win a lawsuit, the scars may never fully heal. When you find yourself facing negative publicity, the first priority is to head it off. Anything you can do, up to the moment a story appears, is probably of more value than everything you may do after that. Reporters make mistakes, and like anyone else, we don't always like to admit them. But we'd much rather do that with a source, than with our readers, listeners or viewers. When we have to make changes, we're more willing to do it before the story appears. Admitting a mistake to you is much less painful than making a public retraction.

A friend of mine realized the importance of prevention, when he called me at home one night, after being confronted by another reporter in my news room. He happened to be the doctor who had delivered my children—and quite skillfully. When my wife delivered twins, he saved her from having to undergo a natural birth *and* a Cesarean section, minutes apart. Now, he was being targeted in a story about unnecessary C-Sections.

He told me he'd had an interview with our investigative reporter, Mark Daly. After the camera was rolling, Mark said he had data indicating that the number of C-sections done by the doctor's group of obstetricians was unusually high. He demanded an explanation. The doctor was taken by surprise and didn't know what to say. Worse, he felt that because he was so unprepared and inarticulate at that moment, he surely looked guilty on camera.

My friend insisted that the data Mark was using was incomplete. He was sure that he could refute it if given a fair opportunity to do so. He wanted me to tell Mark about my favorable experience with him. I told him that as a friend I'd make a call, but I had no way of vouching for his overall practice pattern. It was that pattern that was obviously at issue, not how he delivered my kids. If he had information to refute the story's premise, *he was the one who needed to get on the phone.*

I didn't have any trouble persuading him to do that. He had already begun to gather that material. The media relations folks at the medical center where he had privileges had already contacted our news room to make his case.

My friend didn't get any special treatment from us. He didn't need it, because as it turned out there were questions about the reliability of the data. The story that later aired was still about excessive C-sections done by some doctors, but he wasn't one of them.

Speaking as a fellow journalist, I don't think Mark did anything improper. The doctor had agreed to the interview. He knew what the topic was to be (although he may wish he'd asked more questions beforehand). Mark says the problems that arose with the data were no fault of his own. And like many reporters, Mark was willing to give the doctor an opportunity to follow up on the interview.

Another newsmaker might have given up, deciding that some reporter was "out to get him" and there was nothing he could do. Then when the story aired, it would have been easy to see it as confirmation that reporters are irresponsible and sensationalistic. Sometimes you just need to keep the dialogue going.

The Bad Guys Don't Wear Black Hats.

When someone is caught by surprise, it reinforces the perception that reporters are "sneaky". When we change an intended story, our critics sometimes ask, "Why didn't you have your facts straight?" In reality, we're just trying to sort the "good guys" from the "bad".

We often have only one opportunity to get the pictures we need. It may be a burning building, a body being pulled from a car wreck, or an interview with someone who has broken the law. There may be no way to know whether a death is a murder or a suicide until a day later when the medical examiner completes the autopsy. By that time, it's too late to shoot the scene of the crime. The ethic we usually apply is, "Get the pictures." We can always decide later whether to use them, and we sometimes don't. From our perspective it makes more sense to have something we don't need, than to need something we don't have.

The same holds true for some interviews, in broadcast or in print. If I honestly believe I've found a doctor who is abusing his practice, what are the chances he'll talk to me if I tell him I know that? Who in his right mind would ever talk to a reporter, if he expected to be exposed as someone who is unethical or corrupt? Reporters surprise, or sometimes even ambush people not because we want to make honest people look dishonest. We do it to catch the ones who really are dishonest. In television, that means capturing them on tape.

A reporter in any medium may sometimes need to be secretive. There may be a risk that key documents might be destroyed or important information rendered unavailable if the target of the investigation knows what's happening. There may be a danger that a tipster or other source might be threatened.

Ambush interviews are a widely used weapon in a reporter's arsenal. Some reporters have made them part of their style. Mike Wallace, Dan Rather and Geraldo Rivera have all built their reputations on the technique. If you find yourself on the receiving end of an ambush, and you did what you're accused of, consider yourself caught. For that we make no apologies. If on the other hand, you feel the accusation is false, make your case. Do it on camera as best you can. If you feel that's not enough, continue to make it after the camera has stopped. If you don't have all the facts at your fingertips, say you'll get them and get back to the reporter–then do it.

One bad encounter doesn't have to be the last word.

DON'T PUNISH THE GOOD GUYS.

This is another temptation folks fall into when they think they're dealing with *The Media*. When someone feels mistreated by a reporter, the response is often to lash out at all reporters, refusing to talk to anyone else. The effect of that can be to reward the offender and punish the good guys.

I've watched some very bright people do it. Consider the case of former president of the University of Minnesota, Ken Keller. Keller was caught in a major scandal after spending more than $1-million in university money remodeling his official residence on campus. Eastcliff, as the home is known, was in dire need of refurbishing. The problem was that the money spent to do it was quietly approved with very little oversight. Then when the project ran into major cost overruns, the money was taken from reserves that even the university's regents didn't know existed.

When the true costs became public, Keller–who had been hailed as an academic visionary–suddenly found himself portrayed as a scoundrel. It was an image that local columnists and other members of the media had no small hand in building. The story made great headline material. With each new development, Keller became more and more estranged from reporters. If ever there was a need for damage control, this was it.

One morning, at the height of the controversy, we needed to get his response to calls for his resignation. We called his office and his secretary assured us that he was willing to talk, "Sometime today." Under those circumstances, that was an engraved invitation to camp out on his doorstep, which is what all of us did. Reporters who were covering the story immediately went to his office and waited. We knew we had to be there whenever he might decide to speak.

Before long a member of Keller's staff stepped out and informed us that the president would not be making a statement after all. He was angry, we were told, because a reporter had rudely ambushed him outside his private office. One local television crew had been the first to arrive, and had been ushered into a waiting area. Then the moment Keller appeared, she had pushed a microphone at him.

It proved to be a shrewd move. Her tactic forced him to talk to her, and he was predictably offended. So, she not only got an interview, she prevented her competitors from doing the same. By refusing to talk to anyone else, he was turning it into an "exclusive" for her.

I think he thought the rest of us would decide to leave, but the effect was just the opposite. Instead of sending us packing, his actions increased our resolve to make him talk. He was telling us that it didn't pay to be patient with him. The guy had to go home eventually and we weren't going anywhere! We knew how to do an ambush too, and we certainly didn't like the thought that a competitor was going to have something that we didn't.

Keller kept us waiting for hours, but it must have eventually dawned on him that he couldn't ignore us forever. He finally stepped outside and answered our questions. He, of course, said he had no intention of resigning; soon after, that's exactly what he did.

The facts behind the Eastcliff scandal were such that perhaps no amount of damage control could have saved Keller's job. The strategies that were needed were far more complex than merely dealing with us that morning. Keller apparently felt he had "enemies" among the media. Perhaps he did. But when he identified someone he thought was one of them, he rewarded her for her efforts.

Even the Score.

When someone lashes out at the *The Media* because of one reporter's transgressions, the effect is to *enhance* the value of whatever the offensive reporter obtained. To a journalist, an "exclusive" is the ultimate reward. Instead, reduce the value of those ill-gotten gains. Call a news conference. Invite other reporters, who may not even know about the story until you call. Make sure everyone has the same material, if not more.

Often, it's a reporter's approach that offends you, not what they obtain. If a television crew sneaks pictures of your business, invite another station in for the grand tour. If you're ambushed leaving your own home, call one of the reporter's competitors and offer to do an in-depth interview, and give yourself time to prepare. That way, you're not rewarding the offensive reporter with an exclusive. You're exacting a penalty, by making sure someone else gets a better story.

Keller would have been wise to let the offensive reporter leave, and then welcome everyone else. He could have made sure we got a more detailed response than she did. That would have diluted the effect of her report, and given him a fresh opportunity to look like he was being open. He did finally talk (perhaps after getting some enlightened advice) but he did it so belatedly that the effect was to deepen his rift with the media.

The reporter that nearly cost the rest of us an interview with Keller wasn't always so successful. I know of a grieving family that refused to talk to her or her station because they felt she'd been too aggressive. They spoke with a competitor instead, and made a point of explaining why.

THE PREEMPTIVE STRIKE

Sometimes you know you have a potentially damaging story before any reporter discovers it. Maybe you know a reporter is digging into something sensitive, but it hasn't yet become a story. Don't let events overtake you. Take the initiative. When a female lover threatened to publicly disclose her relationship with tennis star Billie Jean King, King called a news conference and announced it first. Not everyone approved of the relationship, but King was widely applauded for the way she handled the situation.

When health officials learned that a Minneapolis doctor infected with AIDS might have exposed his patients to the HIV virus, they sent letters to all patients who might have been in danger. They planned a news conference, but word of what had happened began to leak out beforehand. So instead of waiting for the story to break, they moved up the public announcement. That way they made sure that all the facts were clear and accurate, and minimized any confusion before any stories appeared. The doctor was identified and his patients were all offered free testing for the AIDS virus to rule out any infection.

It also came out that another local doctor carried the virus. Unlike the first doctor, he had not done any procedures that put patients at risk of contracting HIV. So health officials didn't give his name. They felt obligated to protect his privacy, but reporters aren't so willing to keep secrets. Every news organization covering the story was trying to get the name of the second doctor and in time someone would have. So he didn't wait for a camera to appear at his door. He called a news conference, explained himself and received a great outpouring of sympathy from the public and from his patients.

Each time, doctors and state health officials maintained control of potentially explosive stories. They did it by acting before events closed in on them.

The surest way to discourage reporters from nosing around where you don't want them is to take away the reward for their efforts. Once you've told the story, then there's nothing left to investigate. You've stolen any glory there is to gain from being the first to break the news.

You also gain the opportunity to direct the story to someone who you think may be sympathetic, or who might become sympathetic if given first crack at telling it. I once got a call from a spokesperson for the timber industry, who told me that a competing television station was preparing a story about his employers. It was a story he feared would be negative. He wondered if I would consider doing a story on the industry's positive economic contributions.

I learned from him that every major paper company in the state was considering plans to expand. Collectively, that expansion could total more than $1-billion in new investment, most of it in economically depressed areas of the state. With those kinds of financial interests at stake, it was obvious why he was nervous about any adverse publicity. The piece I did was the lead story of an award-winning show for us.

I never knew what my competitor was working on, and I never saw a story appear. I only know that I got a good story out of it.

Sometimes the only preemptive strike you can make is with your stakeholders. When you know bad publicity is coming, and you can't head it off, you can at least send them a warning. Notify your employees, your major customers or clients, your investors, and your family about a coming adverse story before it shows up in the headlines.

It's not only an important courtesy; it's a good way to ensure that your side of the story is heard by at least those people who matter most.

WHO'S RECORDING WHO?

If you're afraid of being misquoted or quoted out of context, there's one way to help protect yourself: Record the interview. Public figures have been doing it for years. When a governor or the President appears at a news conference, you can be sure that some staff member has a tape recorder rolling, and it's not done secretly. The recorder is often placed right in front, along with everyone else's, and why not? The cameras are rolling; the radio reporters have their tape recorders on; and these days so do many print reporters. Why shouldn't the person talking keep a record of it too? Executives are starting to place small recorders on the table during one-on-one interviews.

There are a couple reasons for doing it. First, it keeps the reporter honest. It eliminates any temptation to embellish what you say. The reporter knows that if necessary you can prove exactly what was said and what wasn't. You have something that you can take to the reporter's boss or even to court, if necessary.

A recording also gives you a way to review your performance. Were you as clear as you wanted to be? Were you quotable? Are there things you can do better next time? Did you leave anything ambiguous, which a follow-up phone call to the reporter might clarify? Broadcast reporters constantly check themselves on tape, to evaluate how we're performing. So should you.

You can also record your phone conversations if you want. A simple device available at any electronics store will allow you to connect your telephone to a tape recorder. However some cautions apply. All states and the federal government have laws regulating wire taps, and there are severe penalties for violating them. To avoid that problem, do one simple thing: tell the reporter that you're recording the call. (And confirm the agreement after the tape is rolling, so you have a record.) As long as all parties to the conversation agree, the recording should be okay.

There's no need to be secretive anyway. The point is to *prevent* any harm from misquotations. Playing "gotcha" with some reporter after a damaging story may have already aired is self-defeating. If you don't have a phone patch when a reporter calls, you can just turn a recorder on next to you. That's generally permitted, and you might as well tell the reporter you're doing it. It will only capture your half of the conversation, but that's the half with all the quotations in it.

Be cautious about recording any conversations in which you go "off the record" or ask not to be quoted. There's something to be said for getting a reporter's assurances on tape, but you'll also be creating a record of what you *don't* want anyone to hear. If you do that, you'd better keep that "smoking gun" in a safe place. And remember, the only way you'll ever prove that a reporter broke a promise not to quote you, is by proving that you really did say it.

YES, WE BEND THE RULES.

I don't have to tell you there are times when reporters act as though we don't have to follow the same rules as everyone else. We expect access to the scene of a crime or accident, beyond what's granted to other passersby. We often have designated parking spaces at public buildings. We expect public agencies to accommodate us in ways they often don't accommodate ordinary citizens. With few exceptions, we assume that virtually all information is public. (Some of us make no exceptions.)

It's an attitude that comes with how we see our job. We argue that we're part of a constitutionally protected institution, that we have the right and the obligation to do whatever's necessary to get at the truth, and then get that truth to the public. What we don't always like to admit is that most of the stories we cover have little to do with the survival of the republic. At any given moment, we're more likely to be responding to our desire to get a good story, than any grand scheme to save Western values. Not being beaten by our competitors is usually a much more urgent priority than the future of democracy.

Just how pure our motives may be in any particular situation is open to debate. The important thing to realize is that some reporters are willing to bend the rules, even break the law to get a story. Don't assume that the law will always protect your privacy. Don't delude yourself into thinking that if a reporter or another source violates the law, that will excuse your actions.

When a Twin Cities I-Team report exposed self-serving practices by a private ambulance company, part of it was based on recordings taken from radio scanners. Reporters were able to document longer response times and lives put at risk. However, the FCC prohibits rebroadcast of such recordings. The station decided the story was worth the cost of the expected fine and aired the recordings anyway.

In another report, the station's I-Team used maintenance records to argue that Northwest Airlines was cutting corners on safety. Northwest countered with the charge that the records had been stolen; that they'd been given to the reporter by a disgruntled employee. It was not very effective damage control. (What about the *planes*?!)

To most people, those sorts of stories justify the means used to get them, but sometimes it's less clear. Like the time the media chased after an advance delegation for Soviet President Mikhail Gorbachev. The group was checking out possible sites for him to visit, but the state officials escorting them wouldn't tell us where.

We wanted to know. So the whole thing turned into a cross between a fire drill and a car rally. We chased them from point to point. Each time the photographers jumped out to get pictures, and jumped back in. We didn't dare lose sight of their van. At one point they tried to lose us. They exited the interstate, only to pull right back on through a metered ramp. I have a confession to make. I didn't wait for that little light to turn green, and neither did the media cars behind me.

Several years ago, a photographer and I followed the Governor's Lincoln with a radar gun. We caught him traveling nearly 20 miles per hour over the posted speed. It was the same day the governor was to decide whether to allow the legal speed limit in the state to increase by half that much. The story got a few chuckles even from the Governor's staff, but not everyone was amused.

A radio talk show host called me the next morning. Some of his listeners thought it was hypocritical of us. They said they'd seen our news vehicles speeding. I assured him that was true and that I had sped in my personal car. I'm sure the same was true of everyone listening. Then I noted that, unlike the Governor, none of us had the power to decide what speed was legal for everyone else.

GUESS WHO?

On a sensitive story, be sure you know the reporter who has called you. If it's someone who's not already familiar to you, do some checking. Make sure they are who they say they are. A professor I know tells me he ended up in the *National Enquirer* after doing a phone interview with a reporter who said he was with *Omni* magazine. He says he discovered the ruse after a reporter who really was with *Omni* later called to do a story about the same research. One easy way to defend against such tactics is to tell the reporter you'll call back. Ask who he or she is with, and in what city. Then *look up the number yourself,* call back through the switchboard and ask for that person. Go ahead and tell the reporter what you're doing and why, and get the reporter's extension if necessary. A reputable reporter won't object, and if it's a disreputable one, you may save yourself the trouble of making the call.

If it's a free-lance reporter, ask for the name of the editor who commissioned the story. If you're told that the story hasn't been sold to anyone yet, get the name of a reputable publication the reporter has worked for previously. If that's not possible, wonder whether you're even talking to a reporter.

You should also be cautious when you're dealing with what I'll call a "surrogate" reporter. It may be a field producer, an assignment editor or someone else whose job it is to assist reporters in setting up stories. Most of the time such calls are routine and harmless. But it can be a prelude to confusion, either accidental or intentional. If someone calls you to set up an appointment on behalf of a reporter, treat them as you would any reporter. Ask the same questions and expect the same sorts of answers. If you feel you need some assurances, be sure you get them from whoever's going to do the story. Ask to speak to the reporter who will be interviewing you, and whoever will be writing the story. Don't assume that the assurances given by one person will automatically be followed by someone else.

BE ESPECIALLY CAREFUL WHEN...

There are certain situations that should immediately raise your antennae, times when you can see trouble coming. One is when you're part of a series. Most television stations do major series only during ratings periods. It's a technique to get more people watching during those months of the year when the size of our audience is being measured. We use series reports to boost those numbers. The results of such "sweeps" determine a station's advertising rates and therefore its revenues for months. Those ratings also determine who will have bragging rights for the largest audience. They're how we keep score.

Our critics argue that any story done for ratings is bad. Personally, I think it's unfair to say that simply because our work earns us money that it's inherently corrupt. (Don't you get paid for your work?) The real issue is to what lengths a reporter will go to get a good story. Some–I'll agree–go too far.

Stations devote considerable resources leading up to sweeps, putting "grabber" stories together. Most reporters consider doing a series to be a plum assignment, because it allows us to do in-depth reporting. But there's also pressure to make that work "sexy", to make it something that viewers will tune in to watch. Such series may be heavily promoted, sometimes in ways that stretch the truth. If you know that what you say or do is going to be part of a series, you will want to be cautious. It can be a great way to get maximum exposure for some problem that concerns you, or it can be a sensationalized attack on you. With a series, there's a greater potential for abuse.

The most common problem is when a reporter's story asserts more than is really there. When four teenage girls were killed in a rural auto accident, an investigative report focused on a man who had allegedly run them off the road. The report was so firm in fingering him, that it "floated" his picture above the girls' graves! The story prompted a special investigation, but that investigation came up with nothing. After reviewing the "evidence" raised in the report, the prosecutor concluded there was no basis for any charges against the man, not even a traffic violation. The man sued.

Investigative reports are almost always done for "sweeps". They're typically little melodramas. There's typically a hero–usually the reporter. There's a villain, such as an unscrupulous auto mechanic or corrupt public official. And there's a victim, perhaps an unsuspecting consumer, an unfairly treated employee or the taxpayers. The viewer at home is given as many cues as possible to cry for the victim, boo the villain and cheer for the hero who comes to the rescue.

Unless you're the one who's tipped off the reporter, or you can corroborate the accusations, you're not likely to be the hero. That role is taken. That leaves only two possibilities, and if you're not a victim, what's left? You may not see yourself as a villain, but avoiding that image can be difficult when you're part of an investigative report. Such stories are *conceived* with certain roles in mind. If there's no villain, often there's no story. But the reporter may have already spent weeks or months on the project.

Frequently, the presumed villain is the last to be contacted, near the time the story is to appear (like my friend the obstetrician). Considerable research, undercover surveillance or interviews with victims may already be done. The reporter will be very reluctant to decide that all that work was wasted. Trying to change the direction of a story at that point, can be like looking for a steering wheel on a train.

Don't let down your guard just because the reporter isn't in television. Radio and print reporters commit the same sins, and generally for the same reasons. A single investigative piece for print may take the better part of a year to complete. Publishers don't allow reporters to do such stories if the result won't sell papers. If you find that you're a target, it's not a hopeless situation, just one that calls for an immediate and aggressive response.

NO SNEAK PREVIEWS

There's one other defensive tactic newsmakers sometimes try. They ask to see the story *before* it airs or goes to press. The answer is *almost* always, "No." Giving in to such a request sets a dangerous precedent and opens up a legal mine field. Still, I have seen it done. Freelance writer David Carr agreed to let Council Member Brian Coyle see the story about Coyle's struggle with AIDS before it was submitted. (Carr says he'll never do it again.) I've also seen it done on stories that might bring lawsuits. I know of a source who was allowed to see how her potentially libelous accusations would appear, to be sure she would stand by those statements.

Unless you've offering a major "exclusive" or your statements are possible grounds for a lawsuit, don't bother to ask. Most news organizations have a strict policy banning any source from seeing a story in advance. It's a stance that's rarely negotiable.

* * *

No matter how skilled or persistent you are, you can't ensure that your relationship with the news media will always go smoothly. (How many things in life do?) If you're a public figure, you're even more vulnerable. As one police chief I know once put it, "One day they're throwing bouquets, the next day bricks." He wasn't talking about public demonstrations. If you're careful, you can be in the headlines without being caught in the headlights. But even your best efforts will sometimes fail. That's why there's another chapter to this book.

CHAPTER 11

CRISIS MANAGEMENT

Crisis Management is what you do when your parachute has failed, your reserve chute didn't open, and you've already bounced once. It's how you react when the missiles have already hit, or you're certain they're about to.

When you've failed to head off bad publicity–or failed to try; when a reporter's actions say, "I'm your worst nightmare," and it's true; even then there's a right way and a wrong way to react. It's still possible to do some damage control.

AFTER YOU GET BURNED

There are times when despite your best efforts, you still get an unfavorable story. When that happens, you need to ask yourself, "Was the reporter unfair?" Or, "Are the facts really against me?" If the facts are against you, you need to look at how to address that problem. If your tanker really did run aground, if you really did steal the money, if what you said really wasn't the truth, then going after the reporter isn't the solution. (Satisfying maybe, but not the solution.)

Pick your battles carefully. I've been part of organizations where management takes "hits" and than refuses to respond when they have a legitimate case to make. They dismiss their critics as hopelessly biased. Then when it keeps happening, they finally decide to fight back the one time when they have the least ammunition.

Determining whether the facts are for or against you determines whether you should attack or retreat. It tells you whether you need to be more assertive or if you'd be wisest to put the whole matter behind you.

When to Attack

Attack is what General Motors did in response to a distorted report about the safety of its pick-up trucks. It's a case that illustrates the lengths a newsmaker may sometimes want to go to set the record straight.

When *Dateline NBC* aired a report on the alleged danger of "sidesaddle" gas tanks on GM pick-up trucks, the immediate effect was devastating to the car maker. A 57-second sequence showed a car crashing into the side of such a truck, and then the truck erupting in flames. The NBC story disclosed that the crash was set up by experts to demonstrate the danger. What the story didn't disclose was that a toy rocket motor was set off under the chassis of the truck moments before the crash, to be sure that any spilled gasoline would ignite. The report also distorted other key facts, including the assertion that the gas tank ruptured, when in reality it hadn't. Instead, gasoline had apparently spilled because of a gas cap that didn't fit properly.

Acting on a tip, GM hired private investigators to search junkyards, found evidence to refute the key facts of the crash sequence, and then called a news conference to announce the story's flaws. It was an expose' which would have made any investigative reporter proud. The counter offensive didn't "prove" the trucks were safe. That wasn't necessary. What it proved was that the story was full of distortions. GM redirected the public's attention to NBC's failings. The network's sins received more attention than the original story had.

When the facts are clearly in your favor, the best approach is to make those facts public as quickly as you can. When a news organization errs as badly as NBC did with that story, there may be a story-about-a-story other news organizations will gleefully help you tell.

When to Retreat

Now NBC had some major damage control to do. But unlike General Motors, the facts weren't in its favor. At first, NBC News President Michael Gartner defiantly dismissed GM's version of events, a reflex response all too often made in such situations. NBC finally came to its senses and did the only wise thing it could do under the circumstances: It admitted that the report was misleading. The lengthy apology was surely written as much by lawyers as journalists. *Dateline* hosts Jane Pauley and

Stone Phillips delivered a long painful "mea culpa" on behalf of the show, the network and those who had done the story.

The statement detailed what NBC had done wrong and explained that the network did not disagree with General Motors' claims. NBC said in effect: We blew it; we know how we blew it; and we're taking steps to make sure that we never blow it in the same way again. It was an admission prompted partly by the fact that GM was preparing to sue, and obviously had a compelling case to make. But it would have been good damage control anyway.

When you're caught with your hand in the cookie jar, don't pretend you're looking for the milk. There are always excuses that you can make, but will anyone believe you? Once you're exposed, it's time to throw yourself on the mercy of the court—in this case the court of public opinion. For NBC to have tried to gloss over its sins would only have further undermined its credibility, credibility which had already been damaged enough.

It's hard making changes because of outside pressures. It's tough to publicly admit that you've done something wrong. Yet that's often what effective damage control demands. A few years ago, animal rights advocates videotaped the mistreatment of "fallen" animals at the stockyards in South St. Paul. The pictures showed diseased animals being dragged around on the ends of chains, like the dead meat they had not yet become. The gruesome images and cries of pain drew national publicity. Company executives responded by calling a news conference, and then outlined a complete change in their procedures for accepting and handling sick animals. The president readily admitted that the media attention was what prompted his company to review its policies. His approach was so forthcoming that the same groups and individuals, who had been most critical, praised the company's response.

Do Your Own Investigation.

In an organization the size of General Motors or NBC, the people at the top may not know the truth without first doing some checking. GM used private investigators, an unusually ambitious step. Much more common is what NBC did. It questioned its own people.

You need to know as much as possible about what really happened, before you decide how to respond. Otherwise you may find yourself prolonging the agony. It's important to correct any inaccuracies and defend your actions if you can. But you don't want to go after a reporter whose only transgression is exposing the uncomfortable truth. That's a futile exercise that will only make you look petty.

Come Clean.

When professional media advisors are called in to do damage control, one of the first things they try to do is get the proverbial skeletons out of the closet. The strategy applies to corporate clients as much as politicians. Before you can determine whether the facts are for or against you, you have to be sure you're looking at *all* the facts. That includes facts that may not be public yet. There's nothing more damaging than having new fires spring up just when you're trying to put out the first one. Is there any as-yet-untold information that will contradict your version of events?

Just weeks before the 1990 election, a newspaper report accused Minnesota gubernatorial candidate Jon Grunseth of skinny dipping with his daughter and several other underage girls at a party some years earlier. He denied the accusations and lingered in the race until more allegations surfaced, about an extramarital affair. The second story would probably never have come out if the skinny dipping story hadn't come first. The alleged affair was newsworthy partly because some of the allegations contradicted Grunseth's statements–statements he had made in his defense following the first story.

The more Grunseth tried to regain his footing, the more he stumbled. When a reporter showed Grunseth a picture of the woman who said she'd slept with him, Grunseth professed not to recognize her. But the reporter could already prove that, at the very least, Grunseth was well acquainted with the woman. The *Star Tribune* newspaper featured an especially damning picture of him squinting at her photograph as if to make out who she was. (Grunseth later insisted that he knew her with a different hair color.) It was a brilliantly timed snapshot. What it portrayed was not so much a lack of fidelity as a lack of credibility. Grunseth was finally forced to step out of the race just two weeks before the election.

Grunseth's partisans took the newspaper to task for making his personal life a campaign issue. The reporters responded that there were still more allegations left unpublished. They said they considered the other charges less relevant, or couldn't fully confirm them. Those of us in the political press corps were amazed that anyone, who appeared to have so much to hide, was so determined to prolong the opportunity for it to come out.

If the pattern here looks familiar, it should. Grunseth was Minnesota's version of Senator Gary Hart. Hart's '88 presidential bid collapsed under the weight of similar "character issues" of infidelity to his wife and dishonesty with the voters. The more Hart tried to explain, the more his explanations got him into trouble. So it was with Grunseth less than three years later.

Candor Disarms.

When an almost identical accusation threatened to undo the '92 presidential candidacy of Bill Clinton, someone finally figured out how to respond. I don't know the whole truth about Bill Clinton's alleged infidelities, any more than you do. But there were two important elements to the damage control he used. One was candor about problems within his marriage. The other was to carefully avoid making statements that someone could disprove.

He said that, yes, he and his wife had had some marital difficulties over the years, and they had resolved them. He avoided adding any' significant new revelations. And he was careful to leave open the possibility that he may have had more than one affair (something that was already rumored, and still is). That's a kind of advance damage control that politicians call "innoculating" yourself. No one could come back to him and say, "You told us this only happened once." An open ended admission like that reduces the incentive for some reporter to probe further. There's no glory in catching someone doing something they've already confessed.

Clinton didn't have to say everything he knew. Had he gotten down to cases, as some interviewers demanded, he almost certainly would have made the story bigger and more damaging. (With who? When?) At the same time, he wasn't loudly proclaiming his innocence. Compare that to Gary Hart's approach. The Senator not only denied that he was having any affairs; he challenged reporters to check him out and prove otherwise. That's exactly what two newspaper reporters did. Hart eventually tried the "coming clean" approach. But he was so late getting to it that he

came across as insincere. By that time, his credibility was
already destroyed.

Senator Hart never recovered, but Clinton did, despite
a barrage of criticism that lasted weeks. The episode was a
major setback to his campaign, but it wasn't fatal. Clinton
not only survived; he went on to win.

Honesty is trump. It can redeem you from all sorts of
sins. When reporters asked Clinton if he'd ever smoked
marijuana, it was his initial *lack* of candor that almost
ended his presidential hopes. His famous, "But I didn't
inhale," remark was so absurd that he was nearly laughed
out of the race. The only way he healed that self-inflicted
wound, was by later admitting that, "It was one of the
stupidest things I've ever said." You can't get much more
candid that.

Few newsmakers will ever face the level of intense
ongoing scrutiny that presidential candidates must handle.
Clinton wasn't just dealing with curious reporters. Like
any politician, he also had plenty of critics eager to point
out his flaws. Still, candor disarmed them, and if it works
in a presidential race, it will work anywhere.

Face Your Accusers.

I keep talking about the need to make your own best
case *before* a story appears (chapters 1, 3, 5, 7, 9 and 10).
The same is true after a story has aired, sometimes more
so. Take the case of Marvin Windows, a company that
found itself in the middle of a political fight it wasn't
prepared to finish. The company was hit with fines for
improper waste disposal practices, and promptly charged,
"Bad business climate." It announced that it was through
creating jobs in Minnesota until the state became more
business-friendly.

The story got considerable play in the newspapers. It looked like the classic face-off between business concerns and allegations of over-regulation by the state. The newly elected governor promptly offered some sympathy to the company, suggesting that perhaps the state's approach to environmental regulation was too adversarial. It was a point he had made during his campaign.

At first Marvin Windows and the Governor seemed to be scoring points, at the expense of the Attorney General's office, which had imposed the fines. That the Governor was Republican and the Attorney General was a Democrat, only added to the controversy. But the AG's office stood firm. It noted that the violations in question were not the first by the company. There had been a number of previous offenses handled administratively by the Minnesota Pollution Control Agency–an apparent pattern of environmental misconduct by the company.

It was at about that time, that I got a call from a local public relations firm. The woman said she was calling on behalf of Marvin Windows. She claimed that some of the news reports were inaccurate, and wanted to be sure that I knew to contact her to get the company's side of the story.

I said, "Great," and asked for an interview with company officials. I suggested that we go to Warroad, let executives air all their complaints, and get pictures of their facilities. I was willing to do an in-depth piece on the issue and their concerns if they would cooperate. She said she'd check with the company and get back to me.

We had a couple more conversations about exactly what I needed, but finally she called and said that company executives had decided to decline my offer. They were afraid that the story would be unfair.

"But you called me!" I said, a little stunned, "I

thought you wanted to tell your side."

"No, I just wanted to let you know to contact me for information," she explained, sounding a little embarrassed.

"It doesn't work like that."

"I know..."

What I didn't say at that point, but should have, was, *"If you're not willing to face the tough questions, don't bother to call."*

The company started out with the right approach. When its executives felt they were getting bad coverage in the newspapers, they tried to correct it. Their public relations firm contacted a different reporter with a different medium. The woman who called me had sought out someone with a fresh perspective. At first, she seemed to be offering access and information to attract my interest—and I was interested. After that final conversation with her, I concluded that the company wasn't willing to be held accountable. It wanted to make attacks and claim that it was being unfairly persecuted. But it wasn't willing to respond to questions about its own pattern of behavior.

It doesn't work like that.

Act Quickly.

One of the first rules of damage control is counterattack before public opinion forms against you. As television has come to dominate the media, those who value their image have learned that the most effective response is an immediate response.

The necessity of a quick response is one of the bedrock assumptions of any modern political campaign. The modern media is so fast and so widespread that any accusation, right or wrong, quickly reaches a vast number of people who will instantly begin forming opinions based on it. The longer a candidate delays answering a charge, the more effort it takes to overcome any damage done. Allow me to draw one more illustration from the 1990 Clinton campaign, because it shows how aggressive a good comeback can sometimes be.

Clinton's campaign staff made the quick response one of its highest priorities, and became quite skilled at it. They didn't want to repeat the mistakes Democratic candidate Michael Dukakis made four years earlier, when he failed to quickly parry away any negative accusations. They were so fast that when South Carolina's Republican Governor Carroll Campbell criticized Clinton as a typical "tax and spend liberal", the response was in reporters' hands before Campbell's words were spoken.

Campbell, who was George Bush's southern campaign chair, was speaking at a Washington news conference. The event had been announced in advance by the wire services. So Clinton's Deputy Campaign Chair, Betsey Wright, dug up an old letter from Gov. Campbell that praised Clinton as "innovative". She also found a newspaper article quoting the Governor, saying that Clinton was "not one of those liberals." Clinton's staff delivered copies of both documents to the reporters covering Campbell's remarks.

Successfully anticipating an attack like that is a rare feat even among seasoned professionals. Clinton had a skilled staff at his disposal, and an archive created for just such a contingency. Few of us have such resources and fewer of us will ever have to worry about how to handle a presidential race. But the same principles apply to anyone faced with adverse publicity.

In many situations, the media attention may be ongoing, lasting days or weeks. The sooner you try to direct that coverage, the greater the impact you'll have. When you're the target of incoming media missiles, you want to change their course when they're launched, not as each one is about to explode.

By delaying, you also risk prolonging the damage. A Minnesota state auditor once did a careful study of teachers' salaries. He concluded that their pay compared favorably to that of middle managers and other professionals with a similar level of education. The Minnesota Education Association, a teachers' union, was upset with the findings. Union leaders thought it overstated what teachers earn. They saw it as a setback in efforts to raise teacher pay. The union criticized the study, but not very aggressively until more than a week later. They then called a news conference to make their counterattack.

There's a problem with that approach. In order to cover the counterattack, reporters had to re-explain the study's findings. For the union, that was like saying, "Okay, you hit me with one missile. Would you please fire another one, so I can try to deflect it?" The union should have stated its objections to the study when it was first released. If you're going to fight back, the time to do it is when your attacker first starts shooting. Don't come up later and say, "Remember how damaging that was to me? Let's talk about it again."

DON'T CREATE YOUR OWN BAD IMAGES

It's tough to ever guarantee yourself favorable news coverage. But it's easy to guarantee that it will be bad.

Certain images and statements are all but irresistible to reporters. The amazing thing is that so many people continue to create them. Here are a few suggestions for getting on the evening news:

Put your hand over the lens of the camera when we're trying to videotape you or someone else.

Better yet, physically push the camera away.

Pull your coat up over your head when the cameras are shooting you being arrested or going into court.

Use profanity to tell us you don't want to talk, or to order us off your property. (We'll probably "beep" it out, but your intent will be clear.)

Stand up and walk out of an interview.

Run from a pursuing camera.

Cry.

That last one might get you some sympathy, but all the others will leave a lasting negative impression. You may not be able to stop a camera from coming after you, but you can control how you act in front of one.

Sometimes the images become the story. Impressions played a major role in bringing down the most powerful woman in Minnesota, the state's first female Speaker of the House, Dee Long. She was a highly respected political leader who was considered a leading contender for the U.S. Senate—until she showed a staggering lack of skill at handling herself around cameras. The harm wasn't all self-inflicted. Long found herself saddled with trying to mop up after a scandal she didn't create. But as events played out, her greatest skill seemed to be taking a bad situation and making it worse.

Reporters dubbed the scandal "Phonegate". It started when House Majority Leader Alan Welle first denied, then tearfully admitted that his son and nephew used the long distance access code that he was assigned as a lawmaker. The teenage boys had shared it with their friends, who shared it with their friends, and so forth until it appeared nationwide on computer bulletin boards.

By the time the abuse was stopped, the calls on just that one code had overloaded the entire state government long distance phone system and run up a tab of some $90,000! Welle apparently didn't know about his son's involvement until after the bills arrived. When he discovered what had happened, he tried to cover it up– even to the point of lying to the newspaper reporters who questioned him about it.

His actions drew plenty of ire from voters, but the damage didn't stop there. When reporters demanded to see all legislative phone records, Dee Long and her staff refused. The political fallout began to spread, not so much because anyone else had abused the system (although some had) but because legislative leaders wouldn't open the books.

Welle resigned, leaving Long to somehow salvage things. Unfortunately, she had already shown an uncanny knack for attracting bad publicity. The day following the Majority Leader's admissions, she managed to get herself caught running away from the cameras–on camera–more than once. After Welle stepped down in a closed-door meeting of the Democratic Caucus, she invited reporters in to discuss what had happened. It was an opportunity to finally display some openness–an opportunity missed. She had barely begun to respond to questions, when members of her caucus shouted, "That's enough, Dee! You don't have to talk anymore." As she got up to leave, they surrounded her with a human wall that looked like something out of the old Soviet Kremlin. Then they escorted her out of the room and into an elevator–all on camera.

Long's missteps with reporters continued until the final act came a few months later. Already badly wounded politically, she ignored the advice of her staff and attended a National Conference of State Legislators in San Diego. While there, she did a little golfing, at an event sponsored by the R. J. Reynolds Tobacco Company, instead of attending some of the meetings. A Twin Cities television crew captured it on tape, just as she had been warned to expect.

That image and the story that went with it finally forced her resignation. It was an outcome so predictable that afterwards even she wondered aloud if she'd had a political death wish.

GET TO "Z".

My friend D.J. Leary does corporate and political public relations consulting. As D.J. puts it, "If you know that the ultimate outcome is 'Z', don't start with 'A B C...'" Go directly to where you know events will inevitably take you and get it all behind you.

When reporters were clamoring for legislators' phone records, the more lawmakers resisted, the more demanding we became. The more they fought any disclosure of those calls, the more we suspected that they had something major to hide. Attorneys for the media had to take the Legislature to court to finally force the release of those documents. Meanwhile, the episode was making headlines day after day.

The logic used to justify keeping the records from us became so twisted that at one point lawmakers argued that we could have the records, but not *yet*! It was as if to say, "We want the daily pounding, that we're getting, to last as long as possible."

When a judge's order finally gave us a look at the phone records, we uncovered a system that was certainly sloppy and lacked oversight. But we found nothing damaging enough to justify such secrecy. The delays did far more harm.

No one was more amazed at how big Phonegate became, and how long it went on, than the reporters covering it. Every story has a certain life expectancy, but this one defied death like Frankenstein's monster. Whenever we thought it was about to fade from the headlines, another delay or blunder would revive it like a lightning bolt into the mad scientist's lab. The story went on for weeks. Then once the phone records were released, it was on the back pages within a couple of days.

It's a phenomenon that's not unique to politics. Anytime you or your company or agency is accused of doing something wrong, we will want to talk to you. The sooner you agree to speak, the sooner we'll stop asking...the sooner you can tell your side...and the sooner the story will run its course. Sometimes the imperative is simply to get it behind you. Make your accusers spend their ammunition. Then assess the damage and decide whether to attack or apologize. Don't prolong the pain.

If there's any doubt about how to respond, err on the side of disclosure. Don't risk having the details dribble out over time. You'll only be creating more incentives for curious reporters to dig, and adding to the perception of a cover-up. If there are more relevant facts that aren't yet public, be the one to disclose them. Turn any unspent bullets into empty shells, so no one can use them against you later. It also gives you first shot at putting a spin on them. A heroic effort to correct a problem can become a bigger story than the original mistake, if it's sincere and it's managed skillfully.

DAY 287 AND COUNTING...

There are times when the crisis can last for days. In extreme cases, like the American hostages in Iran, or a major oil spill, it can last weeks or months. Special Agent Jeff Jamar was the FBI commander at the scene of the Waco standoff outside the Branch Davidian Cult Complex. Few people will ever face such a massive media onslaught.

Jamar has several suggestions for handling such situations. First, he says lay down clear ground rules, and stick to them. (chapter 4.) Have a designated spokesperson, preferably the most senior person available, someone who is both knowledgeable and credible. Then make sure all information goes through that person. If you don't want reporters calling you in the middle of the night, don't give any information to someone who does. You'll only be encouraging more calls. Instead, hold regular news conferences to as he puts it, "Feed the beast." (Reporters call it "spoon feeding".)

Jamar understands something many newsmakers fail to grasp: The reporters assigned to a major ongoing story are responsible for having at least one story *each day*, preferably with periodic updates. If you don't provide enough information to satisfy that appetite, we tend to get a little surly–and we go find it for ourselves. So the more you can say, the more control you have (chapter 3). Reporters always have unanswered questions, but Jamar says local law enforcement officials were stunned by how much the FBI was willing to reveal at Waco.

Keep in mind that reporters have a job to do. If you can accommodate our needs, we'll be more willing to accommodate yours. There are tradeoffs. For safety reasons, Jamar ordered all media well away from the Branch Davidian Compound, but he still allowed them to be within sight of it. When CNN used a night scope to show movements around the compound after dark, the FBI asked them to stop because it was endangering lives. CNN agreed not to show those pictures "live" and Jamar conceeded that it was okay to show them later on tape. After a news conference turned into a shouting match, Jamar demanded that reporters raise their hands and wait to be recognized. He found that most reporters welcome that type of orderly arrangement. We realize that the newsmaker is often the only one able to assume control over such situations.

Jamar advises that organizations prepare for a crisis before it hits. Most businesses have crisis plans to deal with such things as labor problems, accidents or natural disasters. How you'll deal with the media needs to be a carefully thought out part of any such plan.

Above all, Jamar says you need to understand that "media relations" is really "human relations". You're dealing with people, and people generally behave best when there's some structure and stress is kept to a minimum.

COMPLAINING

When news organizations are accused of doing something wrong, we tend to act like any other corporate entity. We do the same things we criticize others for doing. We deny. We stonewall. We try to bury our heads and hope the problem will go away. Even NBC's forthcoming admissions about GM trucks came only after weeks of trying to ignore GM's complaints. We make our living eagerly pointing out the failings of others, and we expect a candid and forthcoming response. Yet we sometimes fail to be candid or forthcoming ourselves. It's a hypocrisy everyone seems to recognize but us.

In every media and at every level, you can find examples of unacknowledged mistakes. You can also find examples of news organizations that genuinely try to make things right. Most newspapers print corrections and many have a reader representative on staff to arbitrate complaints. Television and radio stations have less formal arrangements, but we do sometimes make on-air corrections. At times the best response you can hope to get is a promise that we won't repeat some inaccuracy in future stories. (Not a resounding victory perhaps, but it's better than another poke in the eye.)

What's important is that you make your complaint known. You need to do so quickly, directly and in a way that leaves you above reproach. In other words be as courteous and constructive as you would expect anyone to be with you. You may be pleasantly surprised by the response you get.

Go up the Chain of Command

If you want to gripe about a story, start with the reporter who did it. Then, if necessary go up the chain of command. Often, people will call and ask for the news director or the station manager. Then, when they reach "the boss" they immediately launch into a tirade over a story that the boss may not have even seen. Sometimes, I think executives decide to call a manager, thinking they'll have the greatest influence dealing with their counterpart, instead of the reporter, a mere employee. Advertisers sometimes try to complain through our sales departments.

To be honest, such heavy handed tactics do sometimes work. So don't throw them out of your arsenal. But there are reasons why they shouldn't be the first weapons you choose. One reason is you'll usually be sent back to the reporter anyway. Managers don't want to receive the first call someone makes to complain. In a news room, people are calling constantly with questions and concerns. There are so many that our switchboards keep daily "call sheets" to track them. Managers read those sheets, but they don't want to take all those calls. A news director or editor doesn't know the ins and outs of each story, and doesn't always want to, unless there's a problem. It's much quicker and easier to let the reporter handle it directly.

When the boss refers you back to the reporter, you've probably already lost ground. Think about it for a moment. If a reporter gets a note from his boss saying, "Please call so-and-so about your story on whatever, from last night," the reporter suspects at least two things. One is that you tried to go over his head, which may not sit well. The other is that you've already "spent" some of your ability to appeal the reporter's actions. The reporter knows you already called the boss and it didn't work.

If on the other hand you call the reporter first, you're showing a good faith effort to resolve the problem directly. That alone may help your case. You also have a chance to learn what explanations or counter arguments the reporter will make (to you or to the boss). You still have the threat of appeal. We know you can still go to the editor or news director, or even file a lawsuit.

Most reporters will try to satisfy you, if you approach us in a constructive way. As a source or a potential future source, you're someone we may need. We take calls and we willingly talk about our stories, because that's often how we find more stories. We get plenty of angry calls about stories that are fair, which someone just doesn't like. A call from someone who's sincerely trying to see all sides is often refreshing, and not easy to dismiss. We may be grateful that you're giving *us* an opportunity to explain our actions.

By talking to the reporter first, you have an opportunity to make your case again, to probe the reporter's motives, and maybe learn new things about the story. There's always information we didn't include in a story for brevity's sake. If there are facts we didn't tell our viewers, listeners or readers, there may be things that you don't know—but which the reporter might share if asked.

Sometimes it pays to call even when you're not part of the story. Maybe you feel we should have contacted you. Perhaps you have new information. Call us. It never hurts to put a reporter on notice that you're paying attention to those stories that involve you. We may decide to do a follow up story.

Don't assume.

Don't assume that you know why we did a story a certain way. The reporter may have insights or motives that haven't occurred to you. Our biases aren't as obvious as some of our critics would have you think. I've taken calls from people on one side of an issue, who think I'm against them, when the reality is I personally agree with them. I'm just careful not to be an advocate within the story. A state lawmaker once called me after I did a story on sex education in schools. She had made a very modest proposal in favor of such curriculums and felt the wrath of some parents over it. It was an experience she agreed to share with me and I had included it as an illustration of how sensitive the issue was.

The lawmaker was irate because I had also used some video of a teacher discussing birth control with students. "How could you show a teacher talking about condoms?" she asked. "Now I'll really be hearing from parents!" As a parent myself, I said I agreed with her that kids needed to get some of that information. But I didn't agree with her, if she was suggesting that parents don't have a right to know what's happening in their children's classrooms.

A friend of mine who covered the Minnesota Capitol for a competing television station once got a call from an obviously offended viewer. It was shortly after the '93 session began. Lawmakers had already been chastened by voter impatience with Washington's "gridlock", and didn't want to acquire the same image themselves. So, leaders of the Democratic-controlled Legislature pledged bipartisan cooperation with a Republican Governor and minority lawmakers.

It was a theme the House Chaplain picked up and supported with Bible passages during his opening prayer. Despite the homily and their own pledges, legislative leaders from both parties were soon in a typical partisan squabble. My friend, Art Sasse, decided to inter-cut the Chaplain's remarks with excerpts from the debate, noting how quickly good intentions sometimes fade.

After his story aired, Art got a call from the Chaplain. He asked Art if he thought that was an, "appropriate way to use the Lord's word." Art said he meant no offense. He felt viewers would appreciate the juxtaposition of those passages with lawmakers' actions.

Apparently still not satisfied, the Chaplain probed further,

"Have you ever been to church, son?"

"Just about every Sunday of my life," Art answered. "My father is a Minister."

"Oh."

We Don't Always Know What We're Doing.

There are times when reporters deliberately manipulate the facts of a story, as NBC did. There are other times when we appear malicious but frankly we just goofed.

Years ago, I did a profile on comedian Louie Anderson, as part of a series of reports on local celebrities. The concept of the project was to take each of them back to their school days, so I arranged to talk to him about his high school experiences in St. Paul. Louie admitted having had a rather troubled childhood. It formed the basis for much of his comedy material. He also is much broader of girth than most of us, and he told me how difficult that had been for him as a teenager.

When I first wrote the story, I referred to him bluntly as, "The fat kid." Later, I thought that perhaps that reference was too severe, that it wasn't conveying the sympathetic tone I intended. So I asked the producer who was helping me with the project what she thought of it. She felt it was okay, so I left it alone. But after the story was edited, she memoed me that it came across as, "Quite harsh," after all. I rewrote the passage and the piece was re-cut.

When it came time for that story to appear, neither she nor I nor the editor who had finished it were even in the building. I'll give you one guess which version was shown. Someone simply picked up the wrong tape.

It happens all the time in news rooms. One of the greatest frustrations of any rookie reporter, is dealing with all the ways that even the most carefully constructed plans get screwed up. "Murphy's Law" strikes daily in a news room. In television there are so many technical ways to foul up a story that it boggles the mind. It may be an editing machine that suddenly malfunctions minutes before deadline, "eating" a critical piece of videotape. It may be one weak connection somewhere along a hundred yards of cable that suddenly ends a live report. The result may simply be that a story is lost, but just as often it means that the story's form or content instantly changes. Something that should have been included is left out. A reporter is suddenly forced to ad lib facts that were carefully phrased on tape. A soundbite that was intended to provide balance to the story isn't included.

Human errors are just as common. A producer who's not familiar with the details of a story may write an introduction or a "tease" that completely misstates what the reporter on that story knows to be true. Sometimes reporters just plain get the facts wrong. We're fallible. When we're under pressure, we sometimes do dumb things. A woman who once assisted me at the Capitol went on to work on the assignment desk in our news room. She had demonstrated strong journalistic skills, but was still learning a new position when she faced a "spot news" story. A small plane had crashed at a small town airport near Superior, Wisconsin. Since TV stations in Duluth were much closer than we were, she called our sister station there. They had a crew at the scene well ahead of us and she needed to know what we might be able to get from them. In the excitement of the moment she blurted out, "Do you have video of the plane going down?"

It happens in print too. Space limitations or a late breaking story, sometimes mean that an editor must change a reporter's copy at the last minute. The reporter who wrote it may not approve, but she's already gone home. Some of the most humorous mistakes occur in headlines. Entire books have been written, compiling some of the most absurd examples. One favorite of mine appeared in a Green Bay newspaper above an article about a series of vetoes by Wisconsin Governor Tommy Thompson. Someone failed to put a space between the words "pen" and "is". The result read: "Thompson's penis a sword." Another one in the *St. Paul Pioneer Press* was referring to Minnesota's governor when it read: "Anti-stalking law to protect women sought by Carlson."

Reporters and news rooms make plenty of errors, and many of us are willing to apologize for them or make corrections if you ask. We know that sometimes the best damage control is to admit that we made a mistake and put it behind us.

Getting Satisfaction

Now that I've defended responsible reporters, let me quickly admit that there are also irresponsible ones. We have at least our share of liars and snakes, and if you can nail one, the rest of us will cheer you for it. The reporter who's determined to take advantage of you, in all likelihood made that decision before you were first called. I've tried to give you the insights and techniques you need to defend yourself against unscrupulous tactics, but I don't pretend they're foolproof. The reporter who has a compulsion to deceive you is the most dangerous and at the same time the most difficult to defend against.

Sometimes all you can do is fight back. That may mean demanding a retraction. It may mean threatening a lawsuit. Even when our mistakes are honest ones, you're entitled to have the record set straight. Marshall your facts and go after us.

If you're not satisfied with the way the reporter handles your concerns, then appeal it. Call the reader representative, if there is one. Otherwise, start moving up the organizational chart. Call or write to the editor, the executive producer, or the news director. If necessary, contact the station manager or publisher. I can't give you a definitive chain of command to follow because titles and responsibilities vary from one news organization to another. Just call and ask to speak with the appropriate supervisor. You have a right to expect a response, and most organizations will give you one. If there's one thing we're accustomed to in the news business, it's hearing complaints.

Be clear about what remedy you want. Is it simply the satisfaction of having a reporter or editor say, "I'm sorry."? Do you want the mistake corrected on the air or in print? If you do, say so. But you may not always want that. If the story is damaging and largely true, do you want to revive it because of a minor error? In television and radio, there's no subtle way to make corrections. They inevitably draw more attention to a story. Maybe you just want to be sure the mistake isn't repeated.

Minor corrections are more important with print media, because the story is likely to go into a data base, where an uncorrected error can become part of the "permanent record". It's also possible for a newspaper to run an inconspicuous sentence somewhere, without again drawing so much attention to your problems. Of course, if the mistake is blatant, if someone says you were arrested for child abuse and you weren't, you'll want that proclaimed loudly.

Corrections policies vary widely between different media organizations. As with ethics, you'll rarely find any concrete guidelines in writing. The reaction you get often depends on who you happen to reach, that person's mood, and maybe whether there's a full moon. There's no way to predict what the response will be until you ask.

THE NEWS COUNCIL

If you happen to live in Minnesota (or just recently, Oregon), you may want to use a service that's kind of like a Better Business Bureau for the news media. The Minnesota News Council is an attempt to offer recourse to those who feel they've been wronged by a reporter. Until just recently, it was the only statewide organization of its kind in the country. It has outlived the National News Council, which failed as an early experiment.

Minnesota's council consists of 12 media members from newspapers, television and radio stations around the state, and 12 members representing the public. A state Supreme Court Justice serves as chairman. The council holds periodic hearings on complaints received against news organizations. Whoever's bringing the complaint makes their case before the council; the station or newspaper is asked to respond; and the council then renders a decision to uphold or not uphold the complaint.

There are no punitive measures, only the force of public disclosure that the council thinks a reporter or news organization may have acted improperly. Still, many journalists bitterly attack the council. They say it infringes on their First Amendment rights. Many Minnesota news organizations support the council, through their participation and their financial backing. Others offer only tepid support or strongly oppose it. The council has no power to compel anyone to appear at its proceedings, and some refuse to do so.

When it works, the news council performs a valuable public service. It provides a way for someone to complain about members of the media without going to court. One of the main attractions, for those news organizations who participate, is that it can be a way to avoid lawsuits. To bring a complaint before the council, someone must agree in writing not to take legal action. Another advantage (or disadvantage, according to some critics) is the council provides a forum for complaints that may not justify a lawsuit, but which nonetheless deserve to be heard.

There continue to be discussions about reviving the National News Council. It died for lack of support from the major national media. News organizations such as the *New York Times* simply refused to participate, or actively railed against it. Other states have also considered beginning councils. Some, like Wisconsin, have never been able to overcome media objections enough to start one. Oregon is one state that recently began a news council. There are attempts underway to create similar organizations in Kentucky and Chicago. The Minnesota News Council has on occasion considered hearing cases from out-of-state, but hasn't yet. If you're able to use a news council, I strongly recommend it.

MATTERS OF OPINION

When you feel like punching your fist through the radio, or shredding the morning paper, your outrage may have nothing to do with the facts of a story. The opinions found in an editorial, or that are voiced on a talk show, can be just as irritating, sometimes more so. What do you do? First you make sure that the facts are correct. Even in an opinion piece, you have every right to expect what it says to be accurate. If it's wrong, you should demand a correction just as you would in any other news story.

More often, however, the issue isn't the facts, but rather how someone interprets those facts. Most columnists and talk show hosts strive to be provocative. You need to respond on that level–by voicing your opinion. You can do that with a letter to the editor or by submitting a guest editorial. You can ask to appear on the same talk show to respond (or call in during the show). Or, if the attack is personal, sometimes it's best to arrange for someone else to come to your defense, a friend or colleague.

If you're afraid your response won't be treated fairly, (I know some talk show hosts / wouldn't call), then look for other ways to respond. Try a different show or editorial page. Some companies buy advertising space to run "advertorials". Those are typically essays outlining the company's response to some allegation, or its stand on some issue. However you decide to respond, you need to realize that your critics are just as entitled to their opinion as you are to yours. Make your case, but don't expect it to silence them.

LUKE 14:11

For everyone who exalts himself will be humbled, and he who humbles himself will be exalted.

It's one of those great truths of the ages, and it certainly fits well here. People have an amazing capacity to forgive, but you have to give them the opportunity. If you act like you don't have to answer to some lowly reporter...if you pretend nothing's wrong when the facts say something is, you won't get much sympathy. If you're willing to face scrutiny...if you admit that you've made mistakes and do your best to correct them, people are much more inclined to let you make amends.

When you feel you need to explain things, test those excuses behind closed doors with some trusted associates before you go public with them. Make sure they'll satisfy the skeptics. If your response means calling a news conference, practice taking the questions you expect from reporters. Professional consultants will sometimes grill a client so intensely, that by the time the client faces us, it's a relief. However you prepare, be sure you're saying what you mean and mean what you say. You probably won't get a second chance to redeem yourself. There's no presumption of innocence in the court of public opinion.

If your actions have harmed someone, even inadvertently, *say you're sorry*. Make it a point to sound concerned and sympathetic, whether you believe you're responsible for someone else's misfortune or not. Even when you can prove that you and your organization are not to blame, offer the same condolences you would offer any friend or neighbor, and do it *first*. Then make your case.

When you have a problem that needs correcting, do that correcting as visibly as you can. Make sure your actions are clear and decisive, that they reinforce the message that you want to do what's right. If you act quickly and you're lucky, another story will soon come along to push you from the headlines. If you delay, you risk having such a story push only your response aside, while public attitudes solidify against you. Impressions form quickly.

Finally, as you struggle against the storm, remember another of the great truths of the ages: This too will pass.

EPILOGUE

Like many adults, I took piano lessons as a kid—and didn't stick with it. And like many people who can't play the instrument, I wish I could. Now my kids take lessons, and when friends see the piano in our home, they sometimes ask me if I know how to play. My canned answer is, "Yes, I know how. I just can't do it." I know what the keys are and how to read music. I know where my fingers are supposed to go. I just can't make them go there, because I haven't practiced.

After reading this book, you know how to handle a reporter like I know how to play a piano. You have all the information. Now it's time to practice. Like reporting, it's a hands-on skill. A reporter can learn only so much in a classroom and then we have to go out and make our mistakes. It can be a painful process, especially in a highly visible medium like television. (If you've ever winced over some reporter's stumbles, imagine how the reporter feels.) For us, there's no good substitute for experience, and the same is true for you when you're dealing with us.

A friend of mine is a middle manager for a Fortune 100 company, who's occasionally called on to do interviews. Like most large corporations, his employer has media relations people on staff. So when some reporter calls, my friend says it's common for him to be coached a little before talking. He tells me, "I usually get enough help to give me a false sense of security." What he doesn't get is any comprehensive training on what to do in those situations.

To be sure, many organizations now teach their top level executives what to say in an interview, and such training is starting to trickle further down the corporate food chain. But few executives have much grasp of how to proactively engage the media. They perceive that as a specialized skill, something for the folks in marketing to worry about.

Such attitudes are ironic when you think about what other skills executives must have. Managers get to be managers partly because they can think on their feet. A person's skill at speaking effectively to a group is usually a determining factor in how far someone advances up the organizational chart. Yet when it's time to speak to a bigger audience than would fill any stadium, the perception is that a little coaching will take care of it. Then, when some reporter calls and it's obvious a pre-game pep talk won't be enough, the all-too-frequent response is, "Keep your head down and hope they go away."

Most managers (or public servants...or judges...or school administrators or...) deal with reporters so infrequently that it may seem as if there's little need to know how to do it. It's easier to just hope it never happens. But eventually it will, and even if it only happens once, it can be a disaster—or a heroic success—depending on how you handle it. Few of us would ever attempt to speak before a group without preparing in advance. If your boss says, "Sometime next week I want you to brief the staff on...(fill in the blank)," I doubt that you'll wait until that moment to decide how you'll handle it. So why wait for a reporter's call before you get ready for the biggest audience of your life?

We live in a world in which the media is pervasive. Its presence should always be assumed. But it isn't, even when many other factors are. Organizations routinely consider the potential legal liabilities of a particular action. "Can we be sued?" is a familiar refrain (even among news editors). A company wouldn't dream of manufacturing a new product without first doing some market research to see how well it will sell. But unless the spotlight of public scrutiny is already focused on them, companies and public agencies habitually make decisions with broad public interest, without considering the media implications. Too often the PR department is viewed as a tool to sell or defend decisions that have already been made, instead of providing insight and guidance in making those decisions. So, the image keepers trot out lame press releases justifying the unjustifiable, or they offer incomplete information because the truth can't be told.

By now, you should be much more enlightened than that, and enlightened news sources may be the last best hope for an enlightened media. The experts tell you that you can influence news content through your viewing habits and by what you choose to listen to and read. That may be true, but only in the big picture. For an individual, it's like trying to change the future course of General

Motors by buying or selling a single share of its stock. Your impact is theoretical at best. As a source, you have much more clout. Even as the media hordes descend on you, you have more potential impact on the news than ten or a hundred or a thousand viewers, listeners or readers. Why? Because in the context of that story, you're probably one of only a handful of sources.

Sources are the suppliers of the news business. Who do you think a car maker will listen to most closely: the lone stock holder who doesn't like the latest design; the customer who wants different choices; or the supplier who says he's going to stop sending wheels?

The purpose of this book has been to help you become part of the dialogue. To help you develop the skills needed to meet a reporter at eye level, to make yourself heard, and avoid misunderstandings. Use it. Put it in your desk or your briefcase and refer to it *before* we call you, as well as after. A reporter can be a dangerous foe or a powerful ally, and which one we become often depends on you.

Our enemies already know this stuff. There are villains who are brilliant at media relations, and heroes who are lousy at it. *What we need are skilled and articulate friends.* And if what I've told you helps you weed out some of the shysters among us, all the better. If enough people of integrity and good will learn to understand the news media, and then use what they've learned, we'll all be better off.

I hope I've helped you understand reporters' seemingly mysterious ways. Dealing with us isn't really very complicated. When you get done with all the strategies and counter strategies, the tactics and the techniques, good media relations comes down to this: **Be open and forthcoming; be prepared to answer the tough questions; and speak the truth.**

Good luck. Try not to hit any sour notes.

OTHER RESOURCES

CRISIS RESPONSE, Inside Stories on Managing Image
Under Siege
edited by Jack A Gottschalk, published by Visible Ink
Press, 1993
–Title says it all, contains accounts of one national or
international headline-making crisis after another, as told
by the media relations people who survived them.

THE GREAT AMERICAN VIDEO GAME, Presidential
Politics in the Television Age
by Martin Schram, published by William Morrow and
Company, 1987
–Recounts the ultimate in high stakes media manipulation,
how it's done and how reporters and news organizations
respond.

MEDIA POWER, How Your Business Can Profit From
the Media
by Peter G. Miller, published by Dearborn Financial
Publishing, Inc., 1991
–Excellent insights and detailed advice from a veteran
promoter, a book on "Getting Your Story Told".

MEDIA WRITING, Preparing Information for the Mass
Media, Second Edition
by Doug Newsom and James A. Wollert, published by
Wadsworth Publishing Co, 1988
–A textbook for students of all media, covers both print
and broadcast writing, both news and public relations,
both journalism and advertising, and both fact and opinion.

NEWS TALK I, State of the Art Conversations with
Today's Print Journalists
NEWS TALK II, State of the Art Conversations with
Today's Broadcast Journalists
by Shirley Biagi, published by Wadsworth, Inc.
–Many names you'll recognize, a great way to get "inside
our heads."

PICTURE PERFECT: The Art and Artifice of Public
Image Making
by Kiku Adatto, published by Basic Books, 1993
–A thoughtful and scholarly look at the compelling role
images play in all our lives, and how those images are used
and controlled.

SUING THE PRESS, Libel, The Media and Power
by Rodney A. Smolla, published by Oxford University
Press, 1986
–Not a "How to" book, but a detailed look at how bad
things can get on both sides of the microphone or notepad,
reviews famous cases.

INDEX

279

O

P

Q

R